# THE FUTURE OF ENERGY IN AFRICA

## HEARING

BEFORE THE

### SUBCOMMITTEE ON AFRICA, GLOBAL HEALTH, GLOBAL HUMAN RIGHTS, AND INTERNATIONAL ORGANIZATIONS

OF THE

## COMMITTEE ON FOREIGN AFFAIRS
## HOUSE OF REPRESENTATIVES

ONE HUNDRED THIRTEENTH CONGRESS

SECOND SESSION

NOVEMBER 14, 2014

### Serial No. 113–228

Printed for the use of the Committee on Foreign Affairs

Available via the World Wide Web: http://www.foreignaffairs.house.gov/ or http://www.gpo.gov/fdsys/

U.S. GOVERNMENT PRINTING OFFICE

91–451PDF WASHINGTON : 2014

For sale by the Superintendent of Documents, U.S. Government Printing Office
Internet: bookstore.gpo.gov Phone: toll free (866) 512–1800; DC area (202) 512–1800
Fax: (202) 512–2104 Mail: Stop IDCC, Washington, DC 20402–0001

## COMMITTEE ON FOREIGN AFFAIRS

EDWARD R. ROYCE, California, *Chairman*

CHRISTOPHER H. SMITH, New Jersey
ILEANA ROS-LEHTINEN, Florida
DANA ROHRABACHER, California
STEVE CHABOT, Ohio
JOE WILSON, South Carolina
MICHAEL T. McCAUL, Texas
TED POE, Texas
MATT SALMON, Arizona
TOM MARINO, Pennsylvania
JEFF DUNCAN, South Carolina
ADAM KINZINGER, Illinois
MO BROOKS, Alabama
TOM COTTON, Arkansas
PAUL COOK, California
GEORGE HOLDING, North Carolina
RANDY K. WEBER SR., Texas
SCOTT PERRY, Pennsylvania
STEVE STOCKMAN, Texas
RON DeSANTIS, Florida
DOUG COLLINS, Georgia
MARK MEADOWS, North Carolina
TED S. YOHO, Florida
SEAN DUFFY, Wisconsin
CURT CLAWSON, Florida

ELIOT L. ENGEL, New York
ENI F.H. FALEOMAVAEGA, American
 Samoa
BRAD SHERMAN, California
GREGORY W. MEEKS, New York
ALBIO SIRES, New Jersey
GERALD E. CONNOLLY, Virginia
THEODORE E. DEUTCH, Florida
BRIAN HIGGINS, New York
KAREN BASS, California
WILLIAM KEATING, Massachusetts
DAVID CICILLINE, Rhode Island
ALAN GRAYSON, Florida
JUAN VARGAS, California
BRADLEY S. SCHNEIDER, Illinois
JOSEPH P. KENNEDY III, Massachusetts
AMI BERA, California
ALAN S. LOWENTHAL, California
GRACE MENG, New York
LOIS FRANKEL, Florida
TULSI GABBARD, Hawaii
JOAQUIN CASTRO, Texas

AMY PORTER, *Chief of Staff*     THOMAS SHEEHY, *Staff Director*
JASON STEINBAUM, *Democratic Staff Director*

———

## SUBCOMMITTEE ON AFRICA, GLOBAL HEALTH, GLOBAL HUMAN RIGHTS, AND INTERNATIONAL ORGANIZATIONS

CHRISTOPHER H. SMITH, New Jersey, *Chairman*

TOM MARINO, Pennsylvania
RANDY K. WEBER SR., Texas
STEVE STOCKMAN, Texas
MARK MEADOWS, North Carolina

KAREN BASS, California
DAVID CICILLINE, Rhode Island
AMI BERA, California

# CONTENTS

# THE FUTURE OF ENERGY IN AFRICA

## FRIDAY, NOVEMBER 14, 2014

House of Representatives,
Subcommittee on Africa, Global Health,
Global Human Rights, and International Organizations,
Committee on Foreign Affairs,
*Washington, DC.*

The subcommittee met, pursuant to notice, at 12:59 p.m., in room 2172, Rayburn House Office Building, Hon. Christopher H. Smith (chairman of the subcommittee) presiding.

Mr. SMITH. Good afternoon. The subcommittee is called to order. First of all, let me begin by apologizing for the lateness of convening this hearing. We did have votes on the floor and members are making their way back and I appreciate the patience of our witnesses and guests.

In the 21st century, energy has become vital to modern societies. We all know that. We no longer have to shop for food each day because refrigerators keep food cold and preserve longer, whether in our homes, in restaurants or during the process of trade.

Cell phones, computers, televisions, and other electronics require electrical power to allow us to lead more productive lives in the modern world. As we have seen, even in the Ebola crisis, in an epidemic, it is necessary that medicines and plasma be kept cold so that they don't lose their potency.

Thus, it is both unfortunate and absolutely unnecessary that more than ½ billion Africans, especially in rural areas, live without electricity. Perhaps the great irony is that Africa has more than enough energy capacity to join the rest of the world in utilizing modern technologies that require energy supplies. Approximately 30 percent of global oil and gas discoveries of the past 5 years alone have been in sub-Saharan Africa. Yet, currently, only 290 million out of 914 million Africans have access to electricity. And the total number lacking such access continues to rise. Bioenergy—mainly, fuel, wood, and charcoal—is still a major source of fuel. Hydropower accounts for about 20 percent of total power supply in the region, but less than 10 percent of its estimated potential has been utilized.

This hearing today will examine the current and prospective impact of U.S. Government programs, such as Power Africa and Electrify Africa, as well private international energy projects. I thank our very distinguished witnesses, who I will introduce momentarily, for their leadership in making the dream of the electrification of Africa increasingly a reality.

(1)

Last year, Chairman Royce, backed by Ranking Members Eliot Engel and Karen Bass and I, introduced H.R. 2548, the Electrify Africa Act. This legislation seeks to build the African power sector from increased production to more effective provision of energy. H.R. 2548 passed the House this past May but has not had action yet in the Senate.

Days after the act was introduced, the administration—I am very happy to say—announced its Power Africa initiative and has committed up to $7.81 billion in various types of U.S. technical and credit assistance and other aid to build the capacity of the African power sector.

It seems that every few months, there is yet another discovery of petroleum or natural gas in Africa. Nevertheless, African countries remain net importers of energy. And a distribution of power from the many new sources of energy in Africa remain unfulfilled. This constrains trade and economic progress, social development, and overall quality of life for the people of Africa. Even now, one country, South Africa, accounts for two-thirds of Africa's electricity generation. All of Africa produces less than 10 percent of the energy produced in the United States.

Meanwhile, people across the continent are forced to meet their energy needs by gathering or purchasing charcoal or coal, often putting women in dangerous situations too far from home. Even when such fuels are safely brought back home, their use produces indoor pollution that all too often contributes to sickness and even death. The current situation cannot continue much longer.

Even with 13 percent of the world's population, Africa represents only 4 percent of the world's energy demand. But this situation, thankfully, is changing. According to the report this year by the International Energy Agency, the IEA, since 2000, sub-Saharan Africa has seen rapid growth and a rise in energy use by some 45 percent. So that is a good trend.

We often speak of the rise of the African economies, but for that rise to be truly realized, the rates of power generation and supply must match the growing demand for power. Those cell phones that are transforming all forms of commerce in Africa must be charged. The consumer goods the growing African middle class is purchasing needs electricity. Africans are increasingly unwilling to accept the blackouts and power surges that have made life so difficult for so long.

Africans who have traveled or live somewhere else know this doesn't have to be their lot in life. In fact, even those that don't travel may have seen on TV or heard about that power is available elsewhere and ought to be available to them just like everyone else.

During the colonial period in Africa, countries were limited in their industrialization, but that period has now long passed. It must no longer be used as a reason why African countries are behind in the process of industrialization or power generation.

Today, this lag in power generation is more due to inadequate or unrealistic regulation, lack of finance for significant power generation projects, underinvestment in power generation, even when financing is available, the disconnection of rural populations from national and regional power grids, high cost for energy, and other factors. These obstacles can and must be overcome. They will require additional international collaboration, public-private partnerships, and the will of governments and their citizens. We will not get to the point we believe it is necessary overnight, but we will get there if we take serious measures now and work robustly to bring this about.

With regular electricity, young students will be able to study under electrical light but, also, use computers to advance their studies. Homemakers will be able to keep food fresher with refrigerators and can stretch household income further. And, of course, hospitals—I personally have been in, as well as Greg Simpkins, our staff director for the subcommittee, we have been in so many hospitals where, if it wasn't for a generator, that hospital wouldn't even have a refrigerator that can keep supplies cold as they must remain so, particularly plasma and certain medicines.

Our two panels today will examine international and national programs to achieve regular, sufficient electrical power in Africa and private projects to add to the supply of energy on the continent. The future of energy in Africa is brighter than it has been in the past. But, again, diligent efforts need to be taken; we need to seize the day.

So I want to now yield to my good friend and colleague, Mr. Cicilline, for any comments he might have.

Mr. CICILLINE. Thank you, Mr. Chairman.

And thank you for your leadership. When you say the prospect of energy in Africa is brighter, it is in large part because of your relentless leadership on this issue. So I want to thank you and Ranking Member Bass for your work and for convening this hearing and thank our witnesses for being here today.

It is very obvious that the lack of power available throughout the continent has many negative consequences. It constrains economic growth. It undermines human resource development. It hinders quality of life, progress, and particularly limits the quality of social services and public safety.

So the impact, both on the economic prosperity of the continent as well as on its ability to meet many of the urgent challenges, is severely compromised by the lack of energy. And this hearing will give us an opportunity to really assess the both prospective and current impacts of Power Africa and Electrify Africa. And I am looking forward to the testimony of our witnesses and thank you for being here.

And, with that, I thank you and now defer to the ranking member.

Mr. SMITH. To Mr. Stockman for any opening comments he might have.

Mr. STOCKMAN. Mr. Chairman, I have to tell you, I—on several accounts—or occasions, I was in the Republic of Congo, and unfortunately, there I contracted an unwanted visitor in my body and had to go to the hospital. And that is when I found out the need for refrigeration and the need for antibiotics. And it actually started my journey into trying to ship antibiotics and other medicines to Africa, was my own personal experience of having none and the importance of energy and the importance of having—and, ironically, here is a country, the Republic of Congo, who is, you know, producing quite a bit of oil, yet they didn't have enough oil at that time—I think someone donated lights to them now. When I went back, they actually had streetlights. But they didn't have enough energy to generate electricity.

And the thing that really astounded me, as we were driving down the streets, they filled little Coke bottles full of gasoline and kerosene. You have been over there. You have seen it. And you just marvel at, here is a country that is of great wealth, natural wealth, and yet its own people are very poor and restrictive in terms of what they can get. And it is mind-boggling.

I know, being from Texas, I have 87 refineries in my district. We produce half of all the gasoline in the United States. And I was marveling at the lack of infrastructure for the ability to harvest their own oil for their own needs.

And so, to me, I have always been interested in what a country in Africa has versus what it needs and the confusing outcomes of when you don't have that infrastructure and you don't have that ability to refine and it is unfortunate. I know there is a great deal of what people would call corruption but, on the other hand, the lack of knowledge and how to take their natural resources and make sure it benefits their own people. And it is kind of sad to see that difference. You have great wealth and great poverty, and yet little electricity.

I remember the year I went back there again, and they had, I think the French donated these lights or solar-power lights, so that when you drive down the road now, at least, you have streetlights, and they are individually, ironically, powered by the sun. But the time before they had that, I was driving down there, and the only lights that were in existence in the capital were the lights from the car. And you could see all these people walking in the streets, and the only lights that they had really were from our car lights, which was a little bit alarming.

And I think this is why this hearing is very important. And I think this is why we need to, in the United States, facilitate helping them take their energy, instead of exporting it, but to use it in their own countries.

And with that, Mr. Chairman, I will yield back the balance of my time.

Mr. SMITH. Thank you, to my friend from Texas.

I would like to yield to the distinguished ranking member of our committee, Ms. Bass.

Ms. BASS. Thank you very much, Mr. Chairman, as always, especially for your leadership in calling this particular hearing.

You and I have worked for a long time on this issue and are clear in understanding that one of the most important needs on the continent is building the infrastructure so that the type of trade that you and I would love to see happen can take place.

So I want to thank our distinguished witnesses, including the senior U.S. Government officials from the State Department, USAID, and DOE, as well as energy experts and advocates from civil society. I look forward to hearing your perspectives on the opportunities and challenges of energy resource development in Africa, including an assessment of the economic national security and human development aspects related to the energy sector.

To help address the challenge, we all know that President Obama launched Power Africa last year, which is aimed at doubling access to electricity on the continent. The first iteration of Power Africa sought to provide more than 10,000 megawatts of new, cleaner electricity and increase access to at least 20 million more households and businesses.

Additionally, during the historic U.S.-Africa leaders' summit in August of this year, electrification in Africa was a central point of discussion with African heads of state. In the midst of these talks, President Obama announced a further commitment of $300 million to the Power Africa initiative. And this new commitment would increase the initial pledge of 10,000 megawatts to 30,000 megawatts. And the hope is, is that this creates an opportunity to reach up to 60 million households and businesses.

So, based on these early successes, it is critical that we continue to invest in initiatives that bring increased electricity to the African continent. That is why I was proud to join both chairmen, Royce and Smith, as well as Ranking Member Engel to introduce the Electrify Africa Act. And we are hopeful that that will move forward in the Senate. And so I look forward to today's testimonies and I am interested in what more Congress can do to be of help.

Mr. SMITH. Thank you, Ms. Bass.

I would like to now introduce our three distinguished experts, all of whom have made major contributions in the past and present, who can authoritatively speak to this subject. So we thank you on behalf of the subcommittee for being here.

Beginning first with Mr. Jonathan Elkind, who currently serves as Acting Assistant Secretary for the Office of International Affairs, having previously served as Principal Deputy Assistant Secretary for the Office of Policy and International Affairs from 2009 to 2013. Prior to joining the Energy Department, he worked as a senior fellow at the Brookings Institution, focusing on energy security and other foreign policy issues. He also founded and headed a consulting company, served on the staff of the U.S. National Security Council, and in a variety of other government positions working for the Vice President of the United States, at the U.S. Department of Energy, and at the Council on Environmental Quality.

We will then hear from Mr. Eric Postel who began as USAID's Assistant Administrator for the Bureau of Economic Growth, Education and Environment in March 2011. In October 2014, he was asked by Dr. Shah, the USAID Administrator, to serve as the Assistant to the Administrator for Africa. Mr. Postel brings to the position more than 25 years of private sector experience, working in emerging markets, especially those in Africa. He has also founded an investment banking and consulting firm focused on emerging markets, served as a commissioner of the U.S. Helping to Enhance the Livelihood of People Around the Globe Commission and worked for Citibank Tokyo.

And then we will hear from Dr. Robert Ichord, who serves as Deputy Assistant Secretary in the Bureau of Energy Resources. He is responsible for promoting the transformation of energy systems to achieve greater efficiency and cleaner performance through the use of market forces and innovative financing approaches and leads the Bureau's efforts to reform electricity and power systems and develop more efficient and reliable national and regional electricity markets. Dr. Ichord has a long history of U.S. Government service in the energy field, having worked for the Energy Research and Development Agency, the U.S. Department of Energy, and USAID.

So thank you for being here today, and I would like to begin with Mr. Elkind.

## STATEMENT OF MR. JONATHAN ELKIND, ACTING ASSISTANT SECRETARY, OFFICE OF INTERNATIONAL AFFAIRS, U.S. DEPARTMENT OF ENERGY

Mr. ELKIND. Good afternoon Chairman Smith, Ranking Member Bass, and members of the subcommittee.

I am very pleased to be here to testify on behalf of the U.S. Department of Energy on the future of energy in Africa. The Department of Energy's Office of International Affairs focuses on some of our world's most pressing global energy challenges, from promoting energy security to fostering international collaborations in science and technology, from addressing market volatility to facilitating long-term efforts to mitigate climate change.

We work to leverage the technical expertise of the Department of Energy headquarters and our national laboratories in energy technologies, markets, and policies. So, in that context, I am very pleased, at the interest of the subcommittee in energy development in Africa and propose to sketch some of the major contours in those markets and some of the Department of Energy's activities.

Africa, particularly sub-Saharan Africa, as the chairman noted, is experiencing rapid economic development. Sub-Saharan Africa is the world's second fastest growing region, in fact. The World Bank reports that economic growth rates in sub-Saharan Africa continue to rise, having been 4.7 percent growth in 2013 and forecasted at 5.2 percent for the current year. Thus, many African nations are positioned to become increasingly important, both as energy consumers and as energy producers.

The International Energy Agency, in the report that the chairman referred to, estimates that the sub-Saharan African economy will quadruple in size, growing by 80 percent between now and 2040. Even with robust economic and energy development in coming years, unfortunately, sub-Saharan African countries will struggle to meet the energy needs of their people, unless they can find effective new policies, technologies, and investment, most importantly, to spur sustained energy development. While 950 million people in Africa, according to IEA, will gain access to electricity between now and 2040, over ½ billion will still lack it.

If I turn to oil development in Africa, sub-Saharan Africa has long been an important player in the global oil market, and its role will only grow in coming years. Oil production in the region has doubled since 1990 and now accounts for 6 percent of global production. And, in addition, sub-Saharan Africa accounted for almost 30 percent of oil and gas discoveries over the last 5 years. Sub-Saharan African oil production is projected to grow from 5.3 million barrels a day in 2013 to approximately 6.2 million barrels per day by 2020. At present, more than 80 percent of current production is exported. So with economic growth driving demand for oil and oil products in sub-Saharan Africa, we expect that the region's oil production will shift to much greater domestic use.

On the natural gas front, major new discoveries are generating excitement in global markets and will provide fuel for Africa's growing economies. Among the countries with the most important emerging gas developments are Mozambique, Tanzania, Uganda, and Madagascar, where there have been major progress steps made toward commercial development of newly discovered resources in recent years.

In the power sector, electrification rates in sub-Saharan Africa are unfortunately among the lowest in the world, as has  been noted. North Africa, by contrast, has electrification rates of over 99 percent, but in sub-Saharan Africa, the rates average only 32 percent, meaning that more than 620 million people lack access to modern energy services. And, as the chairman so rightly and appropriately noted, this translates into very concrete impacts on people's livelihoods and indeed their lives.

So, with this context, in 2013, when President Obama underscored the U.S. commitment to Africa's energy development by launching the Power Africa initiative, he also asked for the engagement by the Department of Energy. In June of this year, Secretary Moniz, together with his Ethiopian counterpart, the Minister of Energy and Water, convened a U.S.-Africa Energy Ministerial. It drew together 500 participants, 42 African countries, all the relevant pieces of the U.S. Government, 20 ministers from across northern and sub-Saharan Africa and, importantly, both African and U.S. companies, along with civil society, academia, and other organizations. We focused on clean energy technologies, increased power generation, rural electrification, regional power pools, oil and gas development, policy and regulatory issues, investment opportunities, and the requirements for finance.

In the wake of the African ministerial, the Department of Energy is working with Africa's leading economies to help them meet their energy development goals. I would like to give a couple of quick examples of work that we are doing. In the renewable energy arena, our national renewable energy laboratory is working with Angola's Ministry of Energy and Water to deliver ''Train the Trainer'' program, which will help to make available more instructors and technicians to install photovoltaic systems in Angola.

In the arena of energy efficiency, DOE is working with a number of west African countries through the Economic Community  of West African States to develop an efficient lighting policymakers' toolbox. This will bring together information on lighting standards and labeling and can help raise energy efficiency across that entire region.

In the natural gas arena, in addition to working with the Government of Tanzania to develop natural gas training for university students and government officials, my counterpart, the Acting Assistant Secretary for Fossil Energy, will travel to a series of sub-Saharan African countries in early 2015 in order to engage on the policy environments that are taking shape in some of these critical frontier countries.

The Department of Energy has a strong interest to forge closer links between and among our counterpart U.S. Government agencies and African governments. We also feel it absolutely essential, in view of the investment needs, to work very closely with U.S. companies. We bring to the table particular expertise in regard to energy technologies, markets, and policy. And we view this as a strategic opportunity for the United States, for our companies and also for our partners in Africa.

So the bottom line is this: Energy is the cornerstone of an African strategy for poverty reduction and economic growth, where my colleagues on the panel are more expert to be sure.

DOE, for its part, however, recognizes that economic growth is closely linked, intimately linked to the availability of energy services to meet the needs of African companies and citizens. That is why we are working with private sector and public sector partners, both in the United States and across Africa, to help Africa unleash its full energy potential for the benefit of African citizens and, also, for the benefit of the United States.

Thank you very much for the opportunity to be with you today.

Mr. SMITH. Mr. Elkind, thank you so very much.

[The prepared statement of Mr. Elkind follows:]

**Statement of**
**Jonathan Elkind**
**Acting Assistant Secretary**
**Office of International Affairs**
**U.S. Department of Energy**

**Before the**

**Subcommittee on Africa, Global Health,**
**Global Human Rights, and International Organizations**
**Committee on Foreign Affairs**
**United States House of Representatives**

**The Future of Energy in Africa**

**November 14, 2014**

Chairman Smith, Ranking Member Bass, and members of the Subcommittee, thank you for the opportunity to testify on behalf of the U.S. Department of Energy (DOE) on The Future of Energy in Africa.

The Department of Energy shares the Subcommittee's interest in the energy issues facing Africa. The International Energy Agency (IEA) recently released its Africa Energy Outlook, a special feature in the 2014 World Energy Outlook. The data make clear that with fast-growing economies, expanding populations, and newly-discovered natural resources, African nations will be increasingly important producers and consumers in the global energy sector. Moreover, given the diversity of the African energy sector, it is important to look at distinct regional and national trends in oil production, gas production, and power sector development to adequately capture the energy trends occurring across the continent.

Through a variety of cross-cutting program initiatives, DOE's Office of International Affairs (IA) responds to the most pressing global energy challenges, ranging from energy security and market volatility to long-term efforts to reduce carbon pollution and the impacts of climate change. IA has the primary responsibility for coordinating the efforts of diverse elements in the Department to ensure a unified voice in our international energy engagements, based on data and analysis of energy markets, technologies, and policies.

IA also has lead responsibility for the Department's international activities including those relating to national security, energy security, and international cooperation in science and technology. IA works closely with inter-agency partners, led by the National Security Council. Within the State Department, IA works closely with regional bureaus and the Bureau of Energy Resources. Finally, IA also coordinates DOE's engagement with other Federal agencies, national and international organizations, and the private sector with regard to energy-related entities such as the International Energy Agency, the Asia Pacific Economic Cooperation forum, the Energy and Climate Partnership of the Americas, the Clean Energy Ministerial, the President's Power Africa initiative, and others.

In June 2013, President Obama underscored the U.S. commitment to Africa by announcing the launch of the Power Africa Initiative. In support of the President's message, Secretary Moniz, together with the Energy and Water Minister of Ethiopia, held a U.S.-Africa Energy Ministerial in June 2014 to identify the most critical energy issues facing African countries and develop plans for future cooperation. The Ministerial brought together minister-level attendance from sub-Saharan African and North African countries, as well as senior U.S. government officials, multilateral development partners, regional and sub-regional African energy organizations, academia, civil society, and U.S. and African private sector leaders. The Ministerial provided opportunities for government-to-government, government-to-industry, and company-to-company informational exchanges, and networking on topics such as clean energy technologies, increased power generation, rural electrification, regional integration, oil and gas development, policy and regulatory issues, investment opportunities, and financing.

Following that very successful event, the Department is working with Africa's leading energy economies to address their energy access goals and their ambitions for the growth of their energy sectors. In particular, the Department is developing collaborations with U.S. and African partners to leverage DOE's core competencies in four strategic areas: renewable energy, energy efficiency, safe and responsible oil and natural gas development, and technical capacity-building. These efforts reflect the fact that cooperation with African governments on policy frameworks can help attract energy investment, particularly from world-class U.S. companies and project developers.

In my testimony, I will provide data and analysis of the energy landscape in sub-Saharan Africa, an overview of the Department's activities in the African energy sector, and highlights of our collaborative engagements with other U.S. government agencies.

**The Energy Situation in Sub-Saharan Africa**

Africa is experiencing rapid economic development—sub-Saharan Africa is the world's second fastest growing region, after emerging Asia. The World Bank reports that economic growth rates in Sub-Saharan Africa continue to rise from 4.7% in 2013 to a forecasted 5.2% in 2014.[1] In North Africa, economies grew in 2013 at a rate of 2.6%.[2] Recent economic growth can be attributed to a period of relative stability and security, improved macroeconomic management, strong domestic demand driven by a growing middle class, an increased global interest in Africa's natural resources, population growth, and urbanization. The combination of these factors—fast-growing economies, expanding populations, and newly-discovered natural resources—means that African nations are positioned to become increasingly important producers and consumers in the global energy sector.

---

[1] World Bank, *Africa's Pulse.*

[2] World Bank, *Africa's Pulse.*

Given the global impact of Africa's natural resources, it is helpful to explore three sectors of energy trends in Africa: oil development, natural gas development, and power sector development.

Oil Development in Africa

Sub-Saharan Africa has long been an important player in the world oil market, and it is poised to become even more important. Oil production in the region has doubled since 1990, and now accounts for 6% of world oil production.[3] The region is likely to become increasingly important, since Sub-Saharan Africa accounted for almost 30% of oil and gas discoveries made in the last five years.[4]

IEA forecasts that sub-Saharan African oil production will grow from 5.3 million barrels per day in 2013 to approximately 6.2 million barrels per day before 2020.[5] Sub-Saharan Africa currently exports more than 80 percent of the oil it produces, and since 2000, two out of every three dollars invested into the sub-Saharan African energy sector has been committed to the development of resources for export.[6] However, with increasing demand for oil and oil products in sub-Saharan Africa, the oil production used for export is likely to shift towards domestic use. The IEA projects that demand within sub-Saharan Africa will grow to 4 million barrels per day by 2040, lessening the region's net contribution to the global oil balance.[7]

North Africa's oil production (Algeria, Egypt, Libya, Morocco, and Tunisia), which is currently about 3.5 million barrels per day, is projected to decline modestly by 2040.[8] In particular, Libyan and Algerian crude and lease condensate production is expected to decline from 3.2 million barrels per day in 2010 to 3.0 million barrels per day in 2040, according to IEA International Energy Outlook 2014 data.[9] While potential for growth in Libyan production is high, social and political unrest have hampered production. Algerian production has been slowly declining as a result of amendments to the country's hydrocarbon law which is viewed as unfavorable to foreign investment. The law has since been amended, but increases in investment have not yet been seen.

As a result of the growth in domestic tight oil production since 2008, the United States is importing less crude oil from Africa. In 2008, the United States imported nearly 780 million barrels of crude oil from Africa (approximately 22% of U.S. imports), but by 2013, total annual imports dropped to 236 million barrels (approximately 8.2%).[10] Initially, the majority of U.S. crude imports came from Angola and Nigeria; by 2013, the U.S. imported crude oil from Algeria, Angola, Libya, Nigeria, Chad, Republic of Congo, Egypt, Equatorial Guinea, Gabon, Ghana, and Mauritania. At the other end, Europe has increased its purchases of African crude oil

[3] International Energy Agency, *Africa Energy Outlook.*
[4] International Energy Agency, *Africa Energy Outlook.*
[5] International Energy Agency, *Africa Energy Outlook.*
[6] International Energy Agency, *Africa Energy Outlook.*
[7] International Energy Agency, *Africa Energy Outlook.*
[8] International Energy Agency, *Africa Energy Outlook.*
[9] International Energy Agency, *Africa Energy Outlook.*
[10] U.S. Energy Information Administration.

to replace its own decreasing oil production, and Chinese refinery expansions have also created new markets for African crude oil.

Natural Gas Development in Africa

In addition to the established North African natural gas producers, major new gas discoveries have been made in Sub-Saharan Africa. These significant discoveries of natural gas in East Africa are generating excitement in global markets and Africa's growing economies. Among the countries with emerging oil and gas developments, Mozambique, Tanzania, Uganda, and Madagascar have shown the most progress toward commercial development of newly discovered resources in recent years. The development of these resources will be important to meeting energy needs in Africa and supplying global markets. The IEA projects that Sub-Saharan Africa will make the fourth largest contribution to incremental global gas supply through 2040.[11]

East African countries are exploring natural gas development both for export as LNG and for domestic utilization, including power production and petrochemicals.

Power Sector Development in Africa

According to the International Energy Agency, North Africa's regional electrification rate is over 99%, whereas, in sub-Saharan Africa, the electrification rate averages only 32%.[12] For the discussion of power sector development, I will largely focus on sub-Saharan Africa, where more than 620 million people lack access to modern energy services.

Sub-Saharan Africa accounts for 13% of the world's population but only 4% of its energy demand. Since 2000, energy use in sub-Saharan Africa has risen 45%.[13] Yet, only 290 million out of 915 million people in sub-Saharan Africa have access to electricity. Due to rapid population growth, the total number of people living in sub-Saharan Africa without access to electricity is rising, even as new energy access efforts gain momentum. The IEA estimates that the Sub-Saharan African economy will quadruple in size and energy demand will grow by 80 percent to 2040.[14] Even with robust economic and energy development in coming years, Sub-Saharan African countries will still struggle to meet the energy needs of their people. So while 950 million people in Africa will gain access to electricity between now and 2040, over half a billion people will still lack access to electricity in 2040, according to IEA forecasts.[15]

Sub-Saharan Africa has vast untapped potential in renewables resources, including geothermal, solar, hydro, biomass, and wind, which could make substantial contributions to Africa's electrification goals. However, governments alone will not be able to provide the funding required to meet electrification goals in Africa. Therefore, increased investment from the private sector will be critical. The current estimated annual investment in sub-Saharan Africa's power

---

[11] International Energy Agency, *Africa Energy Outlook*.

[12] International Energy Agency, *Africa Energy Outlook*.

[13] International Energy Agency, *Africa Energy Outlook*.

[14] International Energy Agency, *Africa Energy Outlook*.

[15] International Energy Agency, *Africa Energy Outlook*.

systems is about $8 billion per year. The IEA estimates the scale of investment needed to achieve universal energy access in sub-Saharan Africa will require more than $300 billion by 2030.[16]

**Department of Energy Engagement in Africa**

Understanding the importance of supporting sustainable energy development in Africa, the U.S. Department of Energy is working to bring the capacity of our staff and the national labs to bear in partnering with partner countries throughout Africa to help chart their energy futures. To address the myriad challenges and opportunities in Africa's energy sector, as I noted above Secretary Moniz hosted the U.S.-Africa Energy Ministerial June 3-4, 2014 in Addis Ababa, Ethiopia. Over 500 participants attended the U.S.-Africa Energy Ministerial, with participants from 42 governments, including 22 energy ministers, 5 U.S. government agency heads, and over 50 private sector representatives. The Ministerial featured high-level plenary sessions, a ministers-only meeting, and 10 panel discussions, which addressed the most pressing energy development issues in Africa, including natural gas utilization, mini-grid development, regional power pool coordination, energy efficiency deployment, and technical capacity building through university partnerships.

The Ministerial was a key element of the Administration's efforts to advance critical U.S. energy policy goals in Africa. The forum provided participants with a unique opportunity to share best practices in energy sector development, make policy and project commitments, strengthen energy cooperation, and network with energy infrastructure project financiers and technology providers. By focusing on energy sector growth through private sector investment in Africa, the Ministerial worked to advance the deployment of clean energy and energy efficiency, reduce gas flaring through power generation, foster responsible energy development through use of advanced technologies and industry practices, and grow bilateral trade between the United States and Africa nations.

The Ministerial brought together multiple U.S. government agencies—USAID, State Department, Millennium Challenge Corporation, the U.S. Trade and Development Agency, the Overseas Private Investment Corporation, the U.S. Export Import Bank, U.S. African Development Foundation, and the U.S. Embassy in Ethiopia—in a coordinated effort. Additionally, the U.S.-Africa Energy Ministerial helped facilitate a natural gas-focused Reverse Trade Mission, which was co-sponsored by DOE and the U.S. Trade and Development Agency. The Reverse Trade Mission helped increase demand for U.S. exports, which in turn help create jobs in the United States and provide valuable investment opportunities for U.S. businesses.

As a direct outcome of the U.S-Africa Energy Ministerial, DOE is pursuing cooperative activities with U.S. and African partners in energy efficiency, safe and responsible oil and natural gas development, renewable energy, and capacity building. I'd like to highlight some of our engagements:

Energy Efficiency

---

[16] International Energy Agency, *Africa Energy Outlook*.

• DOE is working with Power Africa and the Clean Energy Ministerial to improve energy access through energy efficiency, looking particularly at mini-grids and super-efficient appliances opportunities and challenges. DOE will host two events in Tanzania in early 2015 focused on increasing energy access in Africa through off-grid solutions + super-efficient appliances, and a technical workshop on a quality assurance framework for isolated mini-grids.

• DOE is working with West Africa nations on an Efficient Lighting Policymakers' Toolbox. This collaborative effort will develop a suite of resources on lighting standards & labeling for energy policymakers in West Africa. The toolbox will include the lighting standards, labeling, monitoring, valuation, and enforcement mechanisms for the West Africa region. Toolbox partners include the Economic Community of West African States, Ghana Energy Commission, Lawrence Berkeley National Laboratory.

Oil and Natural Gas

• DOE is working with the Government of Tanzania on a Natural Gas Training for university students and government officials. The training is planned for early 2015.

• DOE/Fossil Energy Acting Assistant Secretary Chris Smith will travel to emerging oil and gas producing countries in sub-Saharan Africa in early 2015. His efforts will focus on sharing best practices with emerging oil and gas producing countries. The location and partnering organizations are still being determined.

Renewable Energy

• DOE's Office of Energy Efficiency and Renewable Energy is implementing a comprehensive program to spur growth in South Africa's energy efficient and renewable energy market and to create opportunities for U.S. energy efficiency and renewable energy companies in South Africa. Specific activities include policy advising, workshops, pilot projects, and university partnerships. The Comprehensive Renewables and Efficiency Program will be an ongoing initiative, partnering with the Global Cool Cities Alliance and PEER Africa.

• The National Renewable Energy Laboratory is working with Angola's Ministry of Energy and Water to deliver a solar electric train-the-trainer program to increase the number of photovoltaic instructors and eventually solar technicians in Angola and to support the development of an Angolan rural solar electrification program. Solar Photovoltaic Train-the-Trainer Program will be in Angola in late February 2015. The program will partner the National Renewable Energy Laboratory, Angola Ministry of Energy and Water, and Sonangol of Angola.

Capacity Building

• DOE will develop an African continent-wide tool for strengthening energy capacity building, particularly focusing on partnerships between U.S. and African universities.

15

DOE is also an active participant in the interagency Power Africa initiative. Secretary Moniz announced the Beyond the Grid initiative within Power Africa at the June 2014 U.S-Africa Energy Ministerial in Addis Ababa. The initiative focuses on fostering private investment in off-grid and small-scale energy solutions that seek to expand access to remote areas across Sub-Saharan Africa. Beyond the Grid is partnering with over 40 investors and practitioners that have committed to invest over $1 billion into off-grid and small-scale solutions to the underserved market. The U.S. Department of Energy is supporting Beyond the Grid by leveraging the work and resources of three DOE-led initiatives under the Clean Energy Ministerial, a global forum to share best practices and promote policies and programs that encourage and facilitate the transition to a global clean energy economy. These initiatives include the Clean Energy Solutions Center; the Global Lighting and Energy Access Partnership or "Global LEAP"; and, a Quality Assurance Framework for Mini-Grids.

## Conclusion

DOE has a strong interest in working with other U.S. government agencies and U.S. companies delivering technology and policy expertise to support individual country and regional efforts to address the opportunities and challenges presented in the African energy sector. We believe that strategic partnerships are critical to developing effective practices across Africa and accelerating the utilization of clean energy sources and safe and responsible oil and gas development as well as the adoption of energy efficient technologies. These partnerships must leverage African leadership and advance the Administration's focus on trade and investment and clean sustainable energy development in Africa.

In order to secure a more stable global energy future and combat the effects of climate change, we must ensure sustainable management of natural resources and revenues through the development of transparent frameworks. Energy is a necessary cornerstone of an African strategy for poverty reduction and economic growth. DOE recognizes that economic growth in Africa is closely tied to increasing energy access, and we are partnering our expertise and research with African governments to help unleash the full energy potential of Africa for the benefit of African and U.S. citizens.

Thank you and I look forward to any questions you may have.

Mr. SMITH. Mr. Postel.

## STATEMENT OF THE HONORABLE ERIC G. POSTEL, ASSISTANT TO THE ADMINISTRATOR, BUREAU FOR AFRICA, U.S. AGENCY FOR INTERNATIONAL DEVELOPMENT

Mr. POSTEL. Thank you, Chairman Smith, Ranking Member Bass, members of the subcommittee. Thank you for the opportunity to appear before you today.

President Obama's Power Africa initiative and the leadership of Congress, including members of this subcommittee, highlight the extent to which we are all united in addressing one of the core obstacles to Africa's development, the lack of access to electricity. As all of you have noted, without a dependable supply of electricity and an enabling policy environment, the private sector will not invest significantly in African economies. And without private sector investment, local economies, entrepreneurs, and citizens cannot thrive.

Power Africa, a whole-of-government effort by a dozen U.S. Government agencies, is working to address this obstacle. To date, more than 80 private sector partners have committed to invest over $20 billion in power sector development. Power Africa has already helped close deals that will generate more than 3,000 megawatts of energy, providing power for more than 5 million African homes and businesses. For example, with our support, the Nigerian Government privatized 5 generation and 10 distribution companies. These companies, in addition to other planned investments and privatizations, are expected to produce 8,000 additional megawatts of power in the coming years.

At the same time, another member of the Power Africa team, the Overseas Private Investment Corporation, OPIC, has already committed $410 million in financing and insurance to private sector partners' projects. For example, its $250 million financing for the Lake Turkana wind farm in northern Kenya will become the continent's largest wind project when it is complete.

Power Africa focus countries have committed to undertake tough policy reforms in their energy sectors. In August, The Millennium Challenge Corporation, MCC, signed a compact to invest up to $498 million in Ghana's electricity sector. This compact includes tough policy reforms needed to create a viability, sustainable energy sector in order to stimulate private investment. Power Africa has so far been able to catalyze commitments in excess of $4 billion for the development of Ghana's energy sector.

Power Africa's successes extend to U.S. companies as well. For example, General Electric is one of the companies making commitments in that Ghana situation that I just described. As another example, during meetings in a Nigerian trade mission to the United States that was hosted by the U.S. Trade and Development Agency, discussions enabled a company called Itron, a company based in Liberty Lake, Washington, to sell nearly $400,000 worth of electricity meters to Nigerian distribution utilities. And they are discussing right now another order worth upwards of $2.6 million. There is a USTDA sponsored follow-on activities planned that are expected to lead to even more sales by U.S. firms.

Power Africa is also facilitating investment in the small-scale energy solutions that are so crucial to reaching rural communities with no access to the national grids. In September, the African Development Foundation and its partners chose 22 winners of Power Africa's off-grid challenge, a competition that promotes innovative solutions for off-grid energy.

In another small-scale project with an outside impact and an example of something that one of you mentioned, Power Africa is funding the procurement of generators for an Ebola treatment unit and other facilities in Liberia that will power water pumps, lights, and even the washing machines used to clean health workers' hospital scrubs, some of these basic building blocks that we need to help defeat this epidemic at its source.

At this year's African leaders' summit, as mentioned, President Obama renewed our commitment to the initiative and pledged to seek a new funding level of up to $300 million in annual assistance to expand the reach of Power Africa across the continent in pursuit of a new aggregate goal of 30,000 megawatts of additional capacity, thereby, increasing access, if we hit that goal, by up to 60 million households and businesses. Other donor partners also seized the opportunity at the summit to announce major new commitments to Power Africa. Today, as noted before, 600 million Africans don't have access to electricity. Together with our partners in Congress, such as you, our partners in Africa, other donor nations and private businesses, Power Africa is working to greatly increase access to reliable cleaner energy.

Thank you, Mr. Chairman, Ranking Member Bass, and members of the subcommittee for your support and your leadership of this very important initiative. I look forward to your questions today.

Mr. SMITH. Thank you. It is we who thank you for that leadership.

[The prepared statement of Mr. Postel follows:]

**Testimony by United States Agency for International Development
Assistant to the Administrator for Africa Eric Postel
House Committee on Foreign Affairs
Subcommittee for Africa, Global Health, Global Human Rights, and International
Organizations
November 14, 2014**

**"The Future of Energy in Africa"**

Chairman Smith, Ranking Member Bass, and Members of the Subcommittee, thank you for the opportunity to appear before you today.

USAID partners to end extreme poverty and promote resilient, democratic societies while advancing our security and prosperity. Through USAID's new model for development, we are investing in Africa's greatest resource—its people—to sustain and further development, opportunity, and human rights for this and future generations.

President Obama's Power Africa initiative and the leadership of Congress, including Members of this Subcommittee, highlight the extent to which we are all united in aggressively addressing one of the core obstacles to the continent's development. The lack of electricity access has long hobbled Africa's opportunities for durable growth and prosperity. Without a dependable supply of electricity and an enabling policy environment, the private sector will not invest significantly in African economies; and without private sector investment, local economies and entrepreneurs cannot thrive.

Of the 1.2 billion people in the world who have no access to electricity, about half live in sub-Saharan Africa. Yet the region has tremendous untapped sources for sustainable energy generation. Solar, wind, and hydro power resources alone have the potential to meet a large proportion of the continent's energy needs. In addition, East Africa's Rift Valley holds an estimated 15,000 MW of geothermal energy resources, while Tanzania's and Mozambique's proven natural gas reserves are over 100 trillion cubic feet—the equivalent of enough gas to power nearly 100 million U.S. households for 15 years.

Tapping into plentiful, sustainable resources and introducing new energy technologies will advance efforts to mitigate the effects of climate change, and promote economic development and job creation, which in turn can improve quality of life.

Power Africa is helping to make that happen by putting this new model for development into action. In the 16 months since its launch, Power Africa's partnerships with African governments, private investors, other donors, and developers have already begun to bring benefits to the people of Africa and the United States. Power Africa, which is coordinated by USAID and the White House, uses private sector engagements to identify the most critical policy and institutional reform issues standing in the way of electricity generation and access projects. As such, Power Africa does not seek to use American taxpayer money to pay for the construction of large infrastructure; rather, it uses modest amount of funds to facilitate and advance power projects by structuring investment opportunities and opening new markets to companies—from small businesses to multinational corporations.

To date, more than 80 private sector partners have committed to invest over $20 billion in power sector development. Power Africa has already helped to financially close deals that will generate more than 3,000 MW, which has the potential to provide power for more than 5 million African homes, service providers, and businesses. Power Africa is currently considering facilitation of projects expected to generate an additional 15,000 MW of generation capacity.

Our work with the Nigerian Government is among Power Africa's most significant accomplishments of the past year. Although its population is estimated at more than 170 million, Nigeria generates less than 4,000 MW of electricity annually. With legal, financial, and technical support from Power Africa, the Government of Nigeria successfully privatized five generation and ten distribution companies in 2013. As part of their privatization agreements, the generation companies are contractually obligated to increase generation for each plant over the next five years to reach a national total of 6,000 MW of installed capacity. Investments by new independent power producers are estimated to produce another 2,000 MW. Our next body of work is related to the Niger Delta Power Holding Company commencing the privatization of ten generation plants completed or in the final stages of completion under the National Integrated Power Project (NIPP); these are expected to generate another 5,445 MW. This process is stalled, however, due to a lack of access to natural gas, and the investors will not commit the initial payment for the plants until the Government of Nigeria has resolved the issue. To overcome the impasse, Power Africa plans to collaborate with the private sector on a gas strategy for the NIPP projects.

The Overseas Private Investment Corporation (OPIC) has already committed $410 million in financing and insurance to these private sector partners to develop African power projects. OPIC commitments include insurance and $50 million in financing to help construct and operate the massive Azura-Edo power plant in Nigeria, as well as insurance and $250 million in financing to the Lake Turkana wind farm in northern Kenya, which will become the continent's largest wind project when complete. This model of leveraging private investors to lead the way in energy development is at the heart of the Power Africa effort.

OPIC, the Department of State, and the U.S. Trade and Development Agency (USTDA) have also partnered to carry out the U.S.-Africa Clean Energy Finance Initiative, an innovative program to support early-stage renewable energy projects and catalyze private-sector investment in the African renewable energy sector. Game-changing clean power projects that have progressed because of these funds include a Senegalese wind farm which upon completion is expected to provide 150 megawatts of renewable power and a pioneering company that is installing and maintaining thousands of home solar kits across northern Tanzania.

Power Africa's successes extend to U.S. companies as well. To demonstrate the effectiveness of U.S. smart grid technologies, USTDA sponsored a reverse trade mission to the United States for decision-makers from Nigeria's recently privatized distribution companies in November 2013. This reverse trade mission addressed—and targeted U.S. export content for—over $800 million in investments needed in Nigeria, where electricity grids often lose over 40 percent of the power they transmit. The delegates were seeking goods and services that could aid them in their efforts to reduce these losses by more than half over the next five years. As a direct result of these meetings, Itron, a company based in Liberty Lake, WA, recently sold commercial and industry electricity meters to Nigerian distribution utilities. The value of these initial deals is $378,000, and another order worth $2,637,000 is pending. And USTDA is sponsoring follow-on activities to help three of the distribution companies develop comprehensive plans to modernize their networks, which are expected to lead to additional sales for U.S. firms.

The delegates also expressed a strong desire for commercial partnerships with the United States and detailed their countries' efforts to foster better business environments for U.S. companies. U.S. industry participants reported that the visits provided valuable networking opportunities that allowed them to establish new—and strengthen existing—relationships with key African decision-makers, which increases their competitiveness on the continent. USTDA is currently planning follow-on activities, including an aviation conference in South Africa in 2015, to help ensure that U.S. companies are connected to forthcoming transportation and energy projects across Africa.

Power Africa is not only about large transformative projects. Because only 18.3 percent of people living in rural communities in sub-Saharan Africa have access to electricity, compared to 55.5 percent in urban areas, Power Africa launched Beyond the Grid to facilitate investment in small-scale energy solutions. In another example, the Off-Grid Challenge – funded by GE Africa, the U.S. African Development Foundation (USADF), and USAID – is a competition that promotes innovative solutions that develop, scale-up or extend the use of proven technologies for off-grid energy. In September, USADF chose 22 winners from 300 applicants in the second round of the Challenge. These innovative ideas focus on delivering more power for agricultural and commercial activities and include 14 solar projects, six biogas generation projects, one wind turbine system and a small hydroelectricity power plant.

In another small-scale project with an outsized impact, through USAID, Power Africa is funding the procurement of power generators from local suppliers for the Ebola treatment unit at the Island Clinic in Monrovia, Liberia, and other health facilities. The generators power water pumps, lights, and washing machines used to clean health workers' hospital scrubs—some of the building blocks we need to help defeat this epidemic at its source.

In order to become Power Africa focus countries, the governments of Ethiopia, Ghana, Kenya, Liberia, Nigeria, and Tanzania had to commit to undertake tough policy reforms in their energy sectors to improve their business climates, as well as make a concerted effort to attract and leverage private sector resources. Over the past six months, the U.S. government has signed memorandums of understanding with each of these initial focus countries, reflecting their strong and continued commitment to engage in policy and regulatory reform—and progress toward that goal. For instance, in Power Africa countries that are also eligible for Millennium Challenge Corporation (MCC) compacts, before the infrastructure needs are addressed through MCC grant funding, MCC works together with USAID, the State Department, and private sector actors interested in investing to jointly identify structural issues. MCC then requires its partner countries to make the tough policy reforms needed to create a viable, sustainable energy sector. This approach proved successful in Ghana when General Electric credited the compact with being a major factor in GE's plans to build a $1.5 billion, 1,000 megawatt power park and associated infrastructure. MCC's $498 million Ghana Power Compact, signed in August before Secretary Kerry and President John Dramani Mahama of Ghana, has so far been able to catalyze in excess of $4 billion of private sector commitment for the development of the energy sector.

Power Africa's work on energy also extends well beyond the six focus countries, such as through a MCC compact to improve Malawi's power sector and USAID's support of Mozambique's competitive process to tender a wind farm. In addition, OPIC and U.S. Export-Import Bank commitments to Power Africa extend throughout sub-Saharan Africa.

To bolster intra-Africa energy trade, USAID is collaborating with the World Bank Group on developing a list of priority of energy transactions for the West Africa Power Pool, such as generation and transmission from dry gas reserves in Mauritania, transmission links between West Africa Power Pool members, and solar and wind projects in Senegal. USAID is also working with other donors to develop a joint a geothermal strategy for the Rift Valley in East Africa and supporting the East Africa Power Pool, its Independent Regulatory Board, and utilities and regulators from Ethiopia, Kenya, and Tanzania to develop a model "wheeling agreement" that would govern the cost of transmitting power through Kenya.

Power Africa is also working closely with a number of East African countries along with the African Union and other donors to help tap into the region's extensive geothermal resources. USAID recently led a 45-person delegation from East Africa to Portland, Oregon, for the Power Africa-African Union Geothermal Roadshow, where sector leaders from Djibouti, Ethiopia, Kenya, Rwanda, Tanzania, and Uganda met with U.S. Government and private sector officials to discuss potential projects that are ripe for investment and technologies that could advance those projects. Power Africa partners—including Ormat Technologies, Reykjavik Geothermal, and U.S.-based Symbion Power—were able to advance deals in countries such as Djibouti and Rwanda. The Roadshow then travelled to Reno, Nevada, where they visited Electra Therm and Ormat's Steamboat Springs Geothermal facility before returning to Washington for several days of meetings with the International Finance Corporation, the U.S. Energy Association and the private sector. Officials from the African Union Commission, African Development Bank, and the United Nations Environment Program also participated in the roadshow.

The U.S. Government will meet its initial commitment of $285 million for the Power Africa effort, and at this year's U.S.-Africa Leaders Summit, President Obama renewed our commitment to this initiative, and pledged a new funding level of $300 million in annual assistance to expand the reach of Power Africa across the continent in pursuit of a new, aggregate goal of 30,000 MW of additional capacity to Africa, increasing electricity access by at least 60 million household and business connections. The Summit was an historic gathering of more than 50 African heads of state and government, but what set this Summit apart from others was that it provided the opportunity for the leaders to meet with a vast number of American CEOs – many from Fortune 500 companies – forge relationships, and explore mutually beneficial partnerships. Other donor partners also seized the opportunity of the Summit to announce major new commitments to Power Africa:

- The World Bank Group committed $5 billion in new technical and financial support, including loans and guarantees, for energy projects in the six initial Power Africa focus countries.
- The African Development Bank (AfDB) already announced its support to advance Power Africa as an anchor partner, with an initial commitment of $3 billion in the six Power Africa focus countries. Its work focuses on energy production, transmission, and distribution infrastructure, as well as cross-border power pools and policy and regulatory reforms.
- The Swedish government committed $1 billion in grants, loans, and financial guarantees to Power Africa that will focus particularly on clean energy projects, energy efficiency, regional power pools, and access for rural and off grid populations.

Through partnerships with other donors, Power Africa expands the tools to incentivize and advance private sector investment in critical power sector activities. This engagement with other multilateral and bilateral donors also increases Power Africa's scope and reach and creates a unified, coordinated framework among donors for encouraging political reforms.

Today, 600 million Africans do not have access to electricity. Hospitals cannot function optimally. Businesses cannot open and children cannot read after dark. Food rots before it makes it to market. But it does not have to be this way. Together with our partners in Congress, Africa, other donor nations, and private businesses, Power Africa is working to greatly increase access to reliable, cleaner energy in Africa.

Thank you Mr. Chairman, Ranking Member Bass, and Members of the Subcommittee for your leadership and support of this important effort.

———

Mr. SMITH. I would like to now yield such time as may consume to Dr. Ichord.

## STATEMENT OF ROBERT F. ICHORD, JR., PH.D., DEPUTY ASSISTANT SECRETARY, BUREAU OF ENERGY RESOURCES, U.S. DEPARTMENT OF STATE

Mr. ICHORD. Thank you, Chairman Smith, Ranking Member Bass, and subcommittee members. I appreciate this opportunity to discuss Africa's energy future and how we are using our foreign policy tools to support stability and economic development in Africa, to increasing access to electricity, and laying the groundwork for a stable and prosperous energy sector.

I am here representing the Bureau for Energy Resources at the State Department, which focuses on our energy equities around the world and seeks to elevate and integrate them into our broader foreign policy. First, I would like to acknowledge and thank the House for its keen attention to the issue of electricity poverty in Africa, as demonstrated through the passage of the Electrify Africa Act. Clearly, Africa is going through a historic transformation, and the State Department's Bureau for Energy Resources is working hard to help African governments responsibly develop their conventional and renewable energy resources and to accelerate the reform of their electricity systems, which will then encourage private investment, support economic growth, and increase electricity access.

Within our interagency team—and I should say, we have a very, very strong interagency team, one of the strongest in my almost 40 years in government in terms of working on these issues. Within that framework, the Energy bureau is focused on three main areas: One, promoting good governance as it relates to managing oil and gas resources, but this is also very important for the electricity sector as well; second, increasing access to electricity; and, third, increasing the use of renewable energy technologies.

Let me turn to governance. Governance and transparency are key security as well economic concerns. Poorly managed resources can stifle development and feed corruption. With the goal of helping countries avoid these issues, our Energy Governance Capacity Initiative offers governments on-the-ground technical assistance and training, both in the region and in the United States, on some of the most difficult issues facing this sector, for instance, management of revenues, incorporation of best practices into laws and regulations, protecting people and environment from sector impacts.

Under the program we are currently engaged with Liberia, Sierra Leone, Somalia, Tanzania, and the Seychelles. The large offshore gas discoveries in Mozambique and Tanzania, which you are all aware of, have global, regional, and national significance. And we will be working on ways in which we can ensure their sound development as these resources are developed.

Transparency is a key component of good governance, and we are actively involved in the Extractive Industries Transparency Initiative, EITI, to support transparency and accountable management of natural resources. Through EITI, representatives of governments, civil society, and industry work together to produce reports that disclose information about a country's natural resource revenues, allowing the citizens to see how much their natural resources are worth and how they are used. Currently, there are 18 countries in Africa that are EITI compliant and four are EITI candidate countries.

Clearly, we have heard about the statistics on the extent of energy poverty in Africa. And we are not only working through Power Africa, but we are also involved in multilateral efforts, such as the Sustainable Energy for All initiative of the United Nations and World Bank. And we are helping to track investment needed to expand electricity generation, transmission, and distribution, all key sectors.

As an active participant in the Power Africa team, State is focused especially on the policy framework for investment and the reforms necessary to improve the enabling environment and reduce the risk for investors. Through our consistent diplomatic engagement through our Embassies and with African embassies in Washington, the State Department is working to ensure that the transactions, that have been the emphasis of Power Africa, lead to structural policy and governance changes that will encourage even more investment. We have positioned a senior career Foreign Service Officer in the region who is working with our Embassies to enhance and focus our diplomatic efforts while minimizing costs. We are also planning regional training sessions that will upgrade the energy knowledge and skills of our economic officers in the Embassies and in the region.

We are very excited about the Beyond the Grid initiative—the sub-initiative that is part of Power Africa. And we are working globally, as well as in Africa, and looking at promising business and technology models that will help provide energy access to rural populations. And we have helped forge a link recently between Power Africa and the Sustainable Energy for All initiative, with its goal of universal electricity access for the 1.2 billion people around the world, half in sub-Saharan Africa, that don't have access to electricity by 2030. A very ambitious goal, but one that is very consistent with the Electrify Africa and our Power Africa objectives and where the European Union and others are also making large commitments to increase electricity in Africa.

Our power sector program provides expert advice to help strengthen the southern African power pool and the association of energy regulators that oversee this developing market. We see regional power pools as critical to creating the larger markets that can attract investment and tap the diverse resources in Africa. We have our unconventional gas technical engagement program that is working with countries to help them to develop and look at the potentials for their unconventional natural gas resources and do so in a sustainable and safe manner. We are working with many partners around the world, for instance, the International Renewable Energy Agency that has a strong emphasis in Africa, and our initiatives will link with many of theirs and improve the synergy with Power Africa.

In conclusion, Mr. Chairman, sub-Saharan Africa stands at a crossroad. Expansive renewable resources and an emerging oil and gas sector will either be an integral part of bringing light to the continent and lifting it out of poverty or be a catalyst for instability and corruption. We feel the administration and Congress have a historic opportunity to engage across the energy spectrum to address these challenges. I look forward to your questions. Thank you very much.

Mr. SMITH. I thank you very much for your testimony.

[The prepared statement of Mr. Ichord follows:]

**Robert Ichord**
**Deputy Assistant Secretary for Energy Transformation**
**Bureau of Energy Resources**
**November 14, 2014**
**Written Testimony for the House Foriegn Affairs Committee, Subcommittee**
**on Africa, Global Health, Global Human Rights, and International**
**Organizations**

Thank you Chairman Smith, Ranking Member Bass, and subcommittee members. I appreciate the opportunity to discuss Africa's energy future and how we are using our foreign policy tools to support stability and economic development in Africa by increasing access to electricity and laying the groundwork for a stable, clean, and prosperous energy sector. It is a privilege to be joined by my colleagues from the Department of Energy and the United States Agency for International Development (USAID). I am here representing the Bureau of Energy Resources at the State Department, which focuses on our energy equities around the world.

The critical nature of the geopolitics of energy is evident when you look at global oil supply disruptions, which recently have been as high as over three million barrels per day. These disruptions have resulted from reduced output due to political instability in Libya, Syria, Sudan and South Sudan, and politically motivated actions that led to declines in Nigeria and Venezuela, and reductions in Iran's exports by over 50 percent due to effective U.S. sanctions. It is now more important than ever that the United States and the State Department's Bureau of Energy Resources work diligently to ensure that energy resources are used to drive economic growth, stability, and cooperation, rather than conflict. And, at the same time, that we accelerate transformation of energy systems to be more sustainable, reliable, and commercially viable.

Decisions we make today will have long-lasting impacts on the trajectory of a continent on the brink of transformation. I would like to acknowledge and thank the House of Representatives for its keen attention to the issue of electricity poverty in Africa as demonstrated through the passage of the Electrify Africa Act, which underscores that expanding electricity access in Africa is a priority for the U.S. government. Only about 30 percent of the population in Sub-Saharan Africa has access to electricity, with many countries at an even lower access rate.

While the continent faces staggering poverty and severe electricity shortages, it is also characterized by significant economic growth, some of which has been generated by natural resource production. Recent finds of hydrocarbons, particularly in East Africa, stand to help some countries transition from economies focused on subsistence agriculture and dependent on international aid to economies driven by natural resources. Sub-Saharan Africa already has total aggregate daily production of about six million barrels of oil and about an annual 60 billion cubic meters of natural gas. Looking to the future, this area has estimated technically recoverable resources that could total an additional 200 billion barrels of oil and 30 trillion cubic meters of natural gas. For comparison, the United States currently consumes about 19 million barrels per day and produces about nine million barrels per day. In 2013, the United States produced 687 billion cubic meters of natural gas. Africa is similarly rich in renewable resources, with world-class geothermal, solar, wind, and hydropower resources that remain largely untapped.

**Focus of the Bureau of Energy Resources:**

The Bureau of Energy Resources is focused on three broad areas in Africa: increasing access to electricity, promoting good governance particularly as it relates to managing oil and natural gas resources, and increasing the use of renewable energy technology.

Roughly half the people on earth living without electricity are in Africa. Recent projections by the International Energy Agency suggest more people in Africa will live without electricity 15 years from now than do today. Through our work on the Power Africa and United Nations' Sustainable Energy for All (SE4ALL) initiatives, we are helping Sub-Saharan Africa attract the private investment needed to massively and sustainably expand electricity generation, transmission, and distribution.

Poor governance and corruption limit all forms of energy investment and diminish economic development across the continent, and are particularly acute in countries with oil and gas production. We are committed to making sure that the potential for wealth does not cause or exacerbate instability, corruption, and governance problems, and we are focused on ensuring emerging and future oil and natural gas producers have the technical and institutional capacity to manage their hydrocarbons sectors responsibly and transparently for the benefit of their national development.

African governments are showing increased commitment to develop renewable energy resources. The United States and other partner countries and organizations are working with them to assess and develop these resources. The International

Renewable Energy Agency (IRENA), to which the United States is a major contributor, is especially focused on Africa. At the September 2014 Climate Summit in New York, IRENA announced a new step in the Africa Clean Energy Corridors Initiative that will link Eastern and Southern Power Pools and facilitate the development of renewable energy resources.

## Power Africa:

As an integral part of the U.S. Power Africa team, the State Department is giving special attention to the policy challenges facing energy investment and access. Through consistent diplomatic engagement by our embassies in Africa and with African Embassies in Washington, the State Department is working to ensure the transactions which make up the foundation of Power Africa lead to structural policy and governance changes that will encourage investment over and above the 30,000 MW goal.

We have already begun to see progress thanks to U.S. efforts under Power Africa. In Ethiopia, the Corbetti geothermal power plant could eventually bring an additional 1,000 megawatts (MW) online, which would increase Ethiopia's generating capacity by 50 percent. Traditionally, Ethiopia has been reticent to encourage private investment but Power Africa's assistance in facilitating a power purchase agreement (PPA) between the Government of Ethiopia and Reykjavik Geothermal, a private company with U.S. investors, has spurred a reassessment of national policy to make it easier for private companies to invest in Ethiopia.

In Nigeria, Power Africa transaction advisors are working closely with the government to ensure successful completion of the country's ongoing privatization of power sector assets. Regulatory and policy issues affecting power markets, payment collections, and technology must all be resolved for a more reliable and robust electricity sector to develop; issues our assistance is addressing.

Through guidance on policy interventions and technical assistance, ENR supports increased deployment of renewable energy in African electricity grids. For example, in support of Power Africa, the United States and other donors worked with the Tanzanian energy regulator to increase the length of standard PPA for small-scale renewable generation from 15 to 25 years. By guaranteeing revenue over longer timeframes, the new structure allows project developers to demonstrate better cost recovery and lower cost of service, resulting in the dual benefits of lower cost wholesale electricity fees and improved project bankability.

One year after the launch of Power Africa, we are looking at projects supported to date to identify lessons learned and the existing policy frameworks that hinder expansion of electricity access, and what reforms are needed to encourage private investment. The State Department will continue working with the partner governments to implement necessary reforms.

As we enter the second year of Power Africa, the Obama Administration will also increase its focus on populations unlikely to be connected to the grid in the near future. Sixty three percent of people in sub-Saharan Africa live in rural areas and rural electricity access is only 18.3 percent. These communities cannot afford to wait decades before the grid comes to their villages. We are looking at innovative technological solutions that can bring greater prosperity supported to date. From simple solar lanterns to complete solar home systems, through mobile payment solutions for home-based generation and minigrids, there are many new approaches to provide modest amounts of power necessary for rural communities to join a world of economic development and upward mobility.

We are coordinating closely with other Power Africa agencies, including the Millennium Challenge Corporation (MCC) and Treasury to support the institutional and policy changes necessary for expansion of electricity access. The MCC has paid particular attention to this in its Ghana compact which devotes considerable resources to the policy changes needed to support a robust electricity sector.

Through Power Africa's new Beyond the Grid sub-initiative , the U.S. government is placing a renewed emphasis on these types of solutions moving forward. Beyond the Grid focuses on private companies deploying smaller-scale generating technologies to match the scale of distributed resources and the smaller-scale demand of rural and peri-urban communities. ENR will work on identifying unique and promising business models and technologies which, when enabled by smart national policies that support localized provision of energy, can provide high quality access to modern energy services while potentially bypassing the slow pace of centralized reform too often found across the continent.

**Sustainable Energy For All:**

There are many other countries and organizations who share this mission. The United States, led by State/ENR, is playing an active role in the Sustainable Energy For All (SE4ALL) initiative, a multi-stakeholder partnership between governments, the private sector, and civil society. Launched by the UN Secretary-General in 2011, it has three objectives to be achieved by 2030: ensure universal access to modern energy services, double the global rate of improvement in energy efficiency, and double the share of renewable energy in the global energy mix. In Africa, SE4All has identified more than a dozen countries (including five of the six initial Power Africa focus countries) where host governments, with assistance from donor countries, will prepare investment prospectuses and action agendas for increased renewable energy investment.

In Ghana—a Power Africa focus country—ENR leads an SE4ALL multiparty development partner team that works with the Government of Ghana on developing off-grid renewable energy projects by the private sector. As the lead, ENR works with renewable energy project developers and finance organizations to facilitate project implementation. Currently, ENR is structuring a framework for Ghanaian finance organizations to cooperate on project finance while also analyzing the bona fides of project proposals and compiling a project portfolio for consideration by finance organizations. In addition, we played a key role in developing a memorandum of understanding between Power Africa and SE4All, signed in New York in September, to ensure the activities undertaken by these various initiatives are complementary.

## Power Sector Programs and Regional Power Pools:

Additionally, ENR manages a foreign assistance budget that is used in three global energy sector programs: The Power Sector Program, the Energy Governance and Capacity Initiative, and the Unconventional Gas Technical Engagement Program. The Power Sector Program (PSP) supports reform and development in countries in which policy, regulatory, and legal reforms are needed to create the frameworks necessary to attract investment, create long-term sustainability, and increase energy access.

ENR's PSP provides technical assistance aimed at bolstering existing electricity grids, connecting disparate grids within a country, and supporting regional power pools. Regional power pools, which we see as a key component of the future of Africa's energy access, will allow countries to better balance their supply and better address changing electricity demands. For example, in Africa, PSP works to strengthen the Southern Africa Power Pool (SAPP), which will reduce the need for countries to limit exports to their neighbors at times when domestic supplies are tight. Our work in strengthening the SAPP should also help provide more stable electricity generation and provide countries' with the capability to meet growing demand.

ENR is also supporting both the SAPP and the association of national regulators that ultimately will become the power pool's regional regulator. Regionally oriented independent power projects are essential components of a robust regional power trade and full market electrical interconnection. The frameworks ENR is helping to develop will support efforts to harmonize the regional regulatory environment and, in turn, will allow local and international investors to access a larger regional electricity market with increased economic opportunities and reduced financial risks.

In addition to our regionally focused cooperation, ENR, through contractors, helps to design and implement rules and regulations that support private investment in SAPP member countries' power sectors, particularly in new commercially-based power generation projects. These efforts could help countries overcome funding limitations of member governments and state-owned utilities by creating an environment that reduces risk and incentivizes the flow of private capital into the region.

**Energy Governance:**

Increasing access to electricity and responsible management of natural resources are linked goals. Managed well, a wealth of oil or natural gas could help fund or be a component of increased generation capacity. Managed poorly, that wealth could stall or even reverse development.

In many oil producing countries, the sector is rife with corruption and revenue contributes to instability rather than development. Competition for access to and control of energy sources and supply routes can be a source of conflict, and revenues from energy sales can provide funds that prolong conflict. Poor governance of natural resources can also contribute to conflict by allowing pervasive corruption to undermine accountability, hinder economic growth, and encourage civil unrest. This is why ENR sees poor energy governance as a security concern.

One needs only to look to the two largest oil producers in sub-Saharan Africa—Angola and Nigeria—to see the negative impact of a poorly managed oil sector. In Nigeria, the poor oil sector management and oversight is a large contributing factor to the discontent and unrest in the Niger delta. Nigeria also faces oil theft at all levels, from tapping of pipelines in the delta to theft of oil from tankers in the Gulf of Guinea, to theft of oil revenues. The international community has in large part successfully reduced hostage-based piracy off of the East Coast of Africa, but we are now seeing a rise of piracy in the Gulf of Guinea in the West, where oil theft has become an international problem that requires cooperation among the countries bordering the Gulf.

In Angola, the oil sector has made many in the government wealthy while large swaths of the rest of the population struggle with abject poverty. Angola's fuel subsidy program is an example of how poorly managed these funds are. The IMF noted in August that Angola's spending on fuels subsidies amounts to four percent of GDP, about half of the spending in health and education. For example, With only a portion of what Angola spends on depressing gasoline prices below market levels, Angola could finance a conditional cash transfer (CCT) program to reduce poverty among the poorest of the poor. In the absence of serious government commitment to improve the business environment and create the conditions for economic diversification, poverty and inequality remain endemic.

This is a pressing problem in countries throughout the continent. In Somalia, an emerging producer, the presence of oil has the potential to exacerbate tensions between the federal and provincial governments. Uganda and Kenya are expected to begin commercial oil production within the next ten years, while Tanzania and Mozambique have the potential to become two of the largest natural gas producers in the world in the coming decade. Oil and gas exploration is taking place in Liberia, Sierra Leone, Namibia, Madagascar, Ethiopia, Somalia, the Seychelles, and a host of other African countries.

## Energy Governance Capacity Initiative:

Engagement with emerging producers presents an opportunity to establish effective legal and regulatory frameworks, robust financial management systems, and strong environmental and social protections to help these countries transition their economies, expand electricity access, and export their resources without falling victim to the resource curse. Engaging with countries before the resources and revenues start flowing sets a foundation for a well-governed economy that can avoid the serious mistakes that other producer countries have made. Building governance capacity and transparency gives citizens more confidence in their government which contributes to stability and development.

These goals were the basis for the formulation in of ENR's first foreign assistance program, the Energy Governance and Capacity Initiative (EGCI). Formed in 2009, EGCI taps into the U.S. Government's considerable expertise and capabilities to provide assistance that is tailored to the specific needs of individual countries on areas on four assistance tracks related to technical, legal, financial and environmental capacity building issues. ENR also has a contract mechanism to support this work and can deploy in-country advisors and specialized expertise. EGCI works with some of these nascent and rapidly expanding oil and gas producer countries to develop the capacity to more effectively oversee the sector. In Africa, EGCI currently is engaged with Liberia, Sierra Leone, Somalia, Tanzania and the Seychelles. It has previously worked in Uganda and South Sudan and has had diplomatic discussions with other countries, including Namibia and Madagascar.

The EGCI offers governments on-the ground technical assistance and training both in the region and in the United States to help address some of the thorniest issues faced by emerging producer countries. This technical assistance focuses on understanding resources through the most appropriate technologies, responsible management of revenues, embedding international best practices into laws and regulations, and protecting people and the environment from sector impacts.

In addition to conventional oil and gas resources, through its Unconventional Gas Technical Engagement Program (UGTEP), ENR further engages with countries seeking to develop their unconventional natural gas resources – shale gas, tight gas, and coal bed methane – sustainably, safely, and responsibly. In particular, ENR engages with the Government of South Africa as it pursues unconventional gas development as part of its effort to diversify its energy supplies.

**Transparency and Governance:**

Transparency in the sector can empower the public to demand a place in decision-making and a share of the benefits from the extractive sector. Transparency can help expose whether natural resource revenue is being used for the benefit of the people or whether it is being diverted for personal gain or to entrench the existing elite. With sound management, revenues generated by oil and gas can support responsible spending on infrastructure, health, education, and other high-impact sectors, as well as savings for future generations, leading to increased employment and more diverse economic growth.

ENR works with the Extractive Industries Transparency Initiative to support transparency and accountable management of revenues from natural resources. Through EITI, representatives of governments, civil society, and industry work together to produce reports that disclose information about a country's natural resource revenues, allowing the citizens to see how much their natural resources are worth. Currently, eighteen countries in Africa are EITI compliant, and four are EITI candidate countries. Under the auspices of the G7's U.S.-Guinea partnership aimed at strengthening transparency and good governance in Guinea's extractive industries sector, ENR engagement helped Guinea to achieve EITI compliance in July 2014.

More broadly, at the U.S.-Africa Leaders Summit in August, President Obama and African leaders discussed the need for transparency and good governance as essential to development and economic growth. They established a U.S.-Africa Partnership on Illicit Finance, which will create a high-level working group to develop a plan of action to curb corruption, particularly in the extractives sector, and promote transparency in the U.S. and African legal and financial systems.

These are only first steps. We work with foreign governments to identify other areas to improve transparency and management of the oil and gas sectors. We have a regional energy counselor based in Pretoria, who travels all throughout Africa, allowing ENR more physical presence on the continent. Through our embassies, regular interaction with foreign and energy ministries has led to progress on publishing oil and gas contracts. Encouraging governments to establish extractives contract templates and working with international donors to provide governments with negotiation assistance empowers countries to negotiate with oil and gas companies to produce contracts that benefit all stakeholders.

Good governance also includes grappling with questions about balancing potential revenue from exporting oil and gas with ensuring that the resources are used efficiently to help provide electricity to meet both current and future electricity demand. For example, through careful crafting of legislation and through negotiations with oil companies, the Government of Uganda is providing support for an export pipeline while also requiring that International Oil Companies (IOCs) build an oil refinery and power plant in-country, which will eventually process 60,000 barrels per day and provide 50 MW of power. The Governments of Tanzania and Mozambique, where large offshore gas finds have the potential to transform the countries' economies, governments will have to develop new models that take into account the need for revenue, rapidly shifting natural gas markets, current electricity demand, and projected future electricity demand. Natural gas will be an essential element of these countries' electricity sectors in the decades to come, but only with careful planning, increased technical knowledge and capacity, and good governance that elevates the well-being of citizens over the financial and political gains of a select few.

## Conclusion:

ENR's diplomacy spans the globe and extends from addressing oil and gas related-issues to advancing renewables, energy efficiency and access. This is an incredibly exciting time in Africa, where all of the issues that our bureau deals with are at play. Sub-Saharan Africa stands at a crossroads: expansive renewable resources and emerging oil and gas sectors will either be an integral part of literally bringing light to the continent and lifting it out of poverty, or will be a catalyst for descent into instability and corruption. ENR, the interagency, and Congress have a historic opportunity to engage across the energy spectrum to address the many challenges that lie ahead in ensuring a positive outcome.

The role of the State Department's Bureau of Energy Resources on these key energy security and transformation issues is an integral part of our overall diplomacy. We have learned that in an interconnected world, we advance our own energy security and prosperity when our friends and allies advance with us. With the wise stewardship of resources, and by fostering private innovation and investment to expand energy access, we can ensure that the world's energy resources become a sustained driver of growth and stability, and not conflict. I look forward to your questions.

---

Mr. SMITH. I would like to begin with just a few questions and then yield to my distinguished colleagues.

So let me ask you, first of all, what African countries have prioritized electrification? If you could just go through some of those countries. And what are some of the obstacles and challenges that we and others are facing in trying to assist? Are the U.S. and other investments meeting the challenge, or are there gaps? Has enough been allocated to this endeavor to make it happen sooner rather than later?

Operationally, is the emphasis on national governments or state governments or both or local? If you find a national government that is unwilling to be as transparent as we would want them to be, do we look to bypass and go to a state? Because, obviously, in the U.S., it is the States and local governments that carry the heavy burden of providing electricity. Is that model being replicated in Africa?

In terms of the electrification, obviously, we have state-of-the-art electrification here. And I have visited virtually every electricity plant in my State, most of them, not all of them, over the years. They obviously have many environmental safeguards, scrubbers when it is coal, to ensure that what comes out the chimney does not lead to disasters, health-wise, because of pollution. Are those kinds of environmental, sustainable, best practices being incorporated in what we do? It seems to me there is so much on-the-shelf capability and knowledge that it would be a shame if that was lost. If you could just spend a moment on that as well.

Where are the African power leaders, especially the equivalent to the NCO corps, the people who actually run the generators? Where do they get their education? Are they partnering with electricity companies here? Is it something that they are picking up in college? Junior college? Who is training those who will run the plants so that they will be run safely and effectively?

And, finally, the Beyond the Grid initiative under Power Africa is intended to facilitate investment in small-scale energy solutions. Do you think such projects could interest more African entrepreneurs to take a greater interest in creating means to supply energy to underserved communities in Africa? If you could speak to those questions, I would appreciate it.

Mr. POSTEL. Thank you for your questions, Mr. Chairman, and thank you for your leadership on this entire topic and introducing the legislation.

So each country is in a different place, but we have seen a number of countries really focus on increasing electrification. And you see this, for example, as witnessed in the MCC compacts in Tanzania and Ghana. Both governments have realized that the lack of electricity is holding back their growth. I won't go through the whole list, but there are a lot of countries realizing how important this is to their growth, to their healthcare system, to their education system, and are looking to really do a lot more in this area.

There are gaps. Part of the concept behind Power Africa, is to identify what the gaps are and work with the governments and the private sector investors to try to solve them. We have seen cases where private-sector investors from the United States and elsewhere have tried to do deals, and then they run into a roadblock.

And that is where the transaction advisors step in and say, Okay, how do we solve that?

Mr. SMITH. On the gaps issue, is that something you could summarize and provide to the subcommittee, so we get a sense of what you are truly encountering?

Mr. POSTEL. Yes, we can.

Mr. SMITH. And then we could try to be helpful with those governments and——

Mr. POSTEL. We can do that.

Mr. SMITH. Thank you.

Mr. POSTEL. In terms of local and national governance, obviously, there are often national policies that set the energy policy and the tariffs for an entire country. But there are a number of local aspects that also come into play. And we work with all of them in this same roadblock approach to figure out what the challenges are, and how we deal with them.

The question of environmental and social safeguards is very important. And you are absolutely right; we don't need to reinvent the wheel. We need to make sure that, you know, we use state-of-the art. And so all—all the projects—for instance, if there is a component that involves the development banks, each one of those banks has their own policy for checking these things and working with the governments and making sure that the projects fit those standards and don't introduce some really poor practices.

In terms of the education and training, there are local institutions that offer, in some countries, training. In other cases, people have education from the United States or Europe. But it is an area where there are shortfalls. There is actually a longstanding partnership that USAID funds, which involves a lot of U.S. utilities and another one involving U.S. regulators. And they work in combination with people in the individual countries for this very reason so that they could have very technical interactions from one utility technical person to another and to try to increase that skill level because there are definitely gaps, and we need to keep working on that. Similarly——

Mr. SMITH. On that point, if I could. Do those technical people come here to learn, or do our people get deployed there?

Mr. POSTEL. Both.

Mr. SMITH. Oh, both.

Mr. POSTEL. Depending on the circumstances.

Mr. SMITH. How large of an operation is that?

Mr. POSTEL. It is—it is a modest-sized, very economical system where each year we get requests from different countries. And it is not restricted to Africa, but Africa has been a big participant. And then we look at them, and we match them up with different utilities—I don't know off the top of my head but there is probably a utility in New Jersey or some in California. But they match them up with utilities that have the expertise that they need and then they have these exchanges and interactions.

Mr. SMITH. Mr. Postel, for the record, could you provide the committee a sense of what that is?

Mr. POSTEL. Yes, we can.

Mr. SMITH. Maybe a summary. That would be very helpful.

Mr. POSTEL. Yes, we can.

And then, lastly, before I turn to my colleagues, absolutely, on beyond the grid, having local organizations and entrepreneurs seeing the business opportunities is part of the objectives and that is sometimes where some of the credit guarantees of OPIC or USAID or others can help them deal with the risk and introduce them to interesting business opportunities, which they know very well, because some of these remote areas they might know much better than a large company. But I am sure, on several of these points, my colleagues have things to add.

Mr. ELKIND. Thank you.

Chairman Smith, I would add a couple of points, if I may. First of all, we all acknowledge the difficulty of providing broad answers because of the very great diversity of the different circumstances in different African countries and, indeed, rural versus urban settings. But acknowledging that danger, I will attempt to respond.

In regard to the question about cutting-edge development of the power systems, the grid centralized systems, one of the areas that we felt is very, very important and that a number of our agencies have worked on from different vantage points, different perspectives of our respective missions, is the utilization of associated gas from oil development projects. The historical experience of the flaring of natural gas is understandable when infrastructure is lacking but when infrastructure manages to be lacking then for protracted periods of time into decades, then, that is really a critical lost opportunity.

And so one of the things that we have been focusing on in our policy dialogues with African countries and, indeed, one of the things that we are focusing on at the level of identification of mutual interest between U.S. companies and opportunities in certain African countries is this area of gas capture for power generation. Together with the Trade and Development Agency this summer, the Department of Energy organized a reverse trade mission that took leaders from a couple of different African countries to the Houston, Texas, area for a series of meetings with companies involved in gas development, gas sector developments. So we think that there is an area for potential opportunity there.

In regard to the Beyond the Grid initiative and some of the potential for growth with African entrepreneurs, from the Department of Energy perspective, one aspect of this that we have been focusing on is the importance of proper performance of products in the marketplace. It is, of course, easy to spoil the market when you have substandard products, be they for off-grid or for solar lanterns, another area where the Department of Energy has worked. And so we are working with our colleagues at USAID, in particular, to look at this question of how to make sure that off-grid lighting systems, solar systems, and hybrid systems that are a mix of renewables and either diesel or natural gas, that these actually perform in the way that is advertised so that, then, you see a healthy development of that entrepreneurial opportunity going forward.

Lastly, on the issue of the training, I would say from our perspective, this is an area that is a huge interest to U.S. companies. But it is also a key gap. I mean, there is lots of, shall we say, head room, opportunity for growth.

I am sure that members of the committee have had the experience, as I and my colleagues have, for example, as a comparison, of traveling throughout the Gulf region. And when one is in the Kingdom of Saudi Arabia or United Arab Emirates, or Kuwait, many other countries where there have been historical, very long-lasting education and training and company relationships, what that translates into is, not only high quality energy development, it also translates into huge opportunity for U.S. companies because, in many cases, our counterparts are familiar with U.S. standards, U.S. approaches, U.S. vendors. So there is a huge opportunity for growth there. It is an area that DOE is looking to try to develop some ideas on.

Thank you.

Mr. ICHORD. May I make a few points?

Mr. SMITH. Yes. Thank you.

Mr. ICHORD. I have five points that I will chime in here on that relate to the gaps and challenges. The first is a common problem throughout the continent is related to the financial position of the utilities. So one of the challenges is how to strengthen the regulatory environment, the pricing environment and move toward more commercial utilities because, then, the investors will then know that they have a credible off-taker for the power that they are generating. Clearly, we have done a lot of work through Power Africa on power purchase agreements, developing standardized approaches. OPIC has been very active in this area, and that is very important. At the same time, though, you need to have a solvent, financially viable energy system in order to have the long-term investment that is necessary to develop the sector.

Second is, I think, Mr. Elkind's point about the integration of the gas and the upstream issues with the power sector, as a particularly important challenge. Oftentimes you have different ministries, like in Nigeria. And you have got to, in a sense, try to work to help them be a catalyst for them to, at least, try to do better planning so that you can ensure that the oil and gas that is being developed in the country is going to be available to meet the needs of the countries. Ghana is a very interesting example where they want to develop a lot of capacity and yet the oil and gas development has been slow in coming.

The point about urban and subnational, I think, is a very important point in Africa, as well as in other regions because the urbanization process is creating these centers of buildings and industry. And the mayors and the subnational leaders of those entities are becoming more and more important as this process proved. And, as you know, we haven't talked about urbanization, but urbanization is still at really an embryonic stage in sub-Saharan Africa, with less than 50 percent. And even by 2030, you are only going to have 54 percent urban. So there is a lot of—but it is rapidly growing. Working with the cities and the urban areas is a very important area, particularly in areas like energy efficiency.

Fourth area is the entrepreneurial development in local institutions. Here, I think, in many cases, it is very important to work with the local business community, which we are, and also to focus on how we can develop more capacity and receptivity in the local banking system so that they can lend for some of these projects.

41

So it isn't just dependent on international capital coming in because you know that much of the international capital, particularly the private and venture capital, institutional capital, sees huge risks and are very risk-averse in terms of coming into a lot of these areas. So the local banking sector becomes very important. And we have seen in Nigeria and some of the other countries that the local banking system can, if developed, play a key role.

And then, finally, I would say that there are a lot of actors that are playing in this field. I think it is very important. And we, of course, are working very closely with the World Bank and African Development Bank and other donors to try to have a coordinated approach that addresses the range of gaps institutionally and otherwise and that we are trying to leverage our money effectively in that process.

Mr. SMITH. Dr. Ichord, thank you very much.

Ms. Bass.

Ms. BASS. Again, thank you all for your testimony.

As I said in my opening statement, I am a big supporter of Power Africa. But I want to raise a few issues that are raised by others with concern about Power Africa and the implementation.

So I believe, Mr. Elkind, you were mentioning African entrepreneurs. I think you mentioned that. So I wanted to know, to the extent, that the African Diaspora here in the United States was getting involved or what type of outreach are you doing? So a couple of questions, the Africa Diaspora specifically but also just small businesses. You know, I constantly encounter small business people who want to figure out how to be connected and just can't quite make the connection.

You mentioned the reverse trade mission and you mentioned it to Houston. I am wondering if there is any others that are planned? Of course, I am going to make a pitch for southern California, because it seems like reverse trade missions don't quite make it to the West or maybe I am just not aware of them. So that is another issue. And then I want to ask you about the development of the infrastructure on the continent. So why don't I start with those couple of questions.

Mr. POSTEL. Thank you for your questions. I will start, but I am sure my colleagues will add in.

We agree with you that we need to, not only start, but continue with a lot of outreach to reach all different sectors of interested people, small U.S. businesses, Diaspora, large U.S. businesses, and so forth. So we are making progress, but we have more to do.

There are some cases already where there has been Diaspora interest. I understand that there is, for instance, an Ethiopian-American business that is going to be manufacturing smart meters for Ethiopia's electricity company. And I hope that there will be additional successes in the days ahead. And, as you allude to, many members of the Diaspora know very well the business opportunities, and they have, through their own hard work, accumulated capital. And so they are ideally suited to participate in different aspects of this.

And in terms of being connected, we have created a one-stop shop. On the USAID Web site, there is a page. But in the worst case, somebody can just send an email, powerafrica@usaid.gov and then we go, use that one-stop shop to reach out to all the dozen U.S. Government entities involved, depending on what the circumstance is, and make the connections. Because we have the view that people shouldn't have to hunt all over the U.S. Government to figure out who to talk to. So that is why we have created this one-stop shop. We will direct them and save them that trouble. It shouldn't be that difficult for American taxpayers.

Ms. BASS. Well, you know what, I really would like to help you with that as well. So maybe reaching out to Members of Congress, others might want to be involved, African Diaspora, as well African-American Diaspora, who are very interested in participating in Power Africa.

Mr. POSTEL. Thank you. We will take you up on that.

Ms. BASS. Okay. Please do.

Another issue that has come up—and it came up, actually, when the bill was being heard here in committee. And that is, to the extent that as we are in Power Africa, developing—supporting the development of the infrastructure on the continent, to what extent is it getting into communities? So there is some concern from some people that most of the infrastructure is going to be built in cities to help businesses, which is wonderful. But considering that people in the rural areas or even right in the city, in neighborhoods do not have electricity—what always horrified me was the idea of women in childbirth using the light on their cell phone to deliver a baby. So I am wondering about that.

Mr. ICHORD. Let me start. Clearly, the issues related to the models for rural electrification are changing a lot. I mean, it is really a revolution that is occurring in which the drop in prices for solar systems, the advances in telecommunications and cell phones—I just came back from Bangladesh—some of the models and commercial approaches that are being taken, I think, are going to be extremely important for Africa because you have such large rural populations without access. You have small—relatively small loads. The economics of extending the grid by utilities that don't have the money to do it, you know, or don't necessarily have the same kind of commitment to extend the systems because they are, in many cases, struggling to just meet urban requirements.

Ms. BASS. And, in urban, I was referring to in neighborhoods——

Mr. ICHORD. In neighborhoods. Yeah.

Ms. BASS [continuing]. In urban communities that——

Mr. ICHORD. So—but I think—I think——

Ms. BASS [continuing]. Commercial areas.

Mr. ICHORD [continuing]. The issue is related to—you know, to decentralized approaches that are relevant to some of the urban areas as well as to the rural areas.

Ms. BASS. Right. So so what——

Mr. ICHORD. And I think there was, also, your question about the entrepreneurial opportunities to work with U.S. companies——

Ms. BASS. Right.

Mr. ICHORD [continuing]. Who are at the—at the leading edge of these technologies. We are working with a California company that has developed a nanogrid approach in Bangladesh and that is the kind of innovation that I see going on in the U.S.—with the U.S.

companies that we can begin to try to focus on to take a closer look at Africa and the market opportunities there.

Ms. BASS. So you are telling me that it is a part of the initiative?

Mr. ICHORD. Well, I think that is why I said we are excited about Beyond the Grid because, in a sense, we are in the early stages here. But a lot of companies have come up and expressed interest in involvement. And I think that, if we get the right strategies, we can indeed help accelerate the commercialization of these kinds of options for Africa.

Ms. BASS. And maybe you can, you know, at another point, give me the name of that company in California.

Mr. ICHORD. Sure. Will do.

Ms. BASS. So a couple of other areas. Another area of concern that gets raised a lot is to what extent is Power Africa looking at renewables? As you know, that is always a controversial issue, whether Power Africa is just going to focus on fossil fuels. So to what extent? From anybody. And then I have one final question after that.

Mr. ELKIND. Ranking Member Bass, thank you for those questions. Just to respond to a couple of the ones that you have posed.

First of all, in relation to the reverse trade missions, we would be happy to go back and talk with our colleagues at the Trade and Development Agency that lead in the organization of them. Our agency and others from across the U.S. Government typically provide technical depth and some of the relationships with the companies that can help to make them most effective. But I will be happy to take away yur interest in knowing what more do they have planned over the horizon.

Ms. BASS. Well, good. You are going to tell them to come to Los Angeles, then, huh?

Mr. ELKIND. I beg your pardon?

Ms. BASS. Are you going to tell them to come to Los Angeles?

Mr. ELKIND. Well, I am told that——

Ms. BASS. I'm just kidding.

Mr. ELKIND [continuing]. In fact, there is a TDA representative in Los Angeles that is working on an effort called Making Global Local to get reverse trade missions to cities across the United States. So some of that may, in fact, be happening and we will provide you more——

Ms. BASS. And I am sorry. Tell me the name of it again. What did you say?

Mr. ELKIND. Making Global Local.

Ms. BASS. Oh, okay.

Mr. ELKIND. So, indeed, some of this may be happening, and we will get the details back to you for the record.

Concerning the role of renewables in Power Africa, I mean, the first point—the approach that we, as an administration, are taking is very nonspecific as to technologies. There are going to be different answers that work in different contexts.

Ms. BASS. Great.

Mr. ELKIND. Beyond the Grid is all about figuring out where there are opportunities, be it for renewable systems with storage, hybrid systems that involve a mix of renewables and fossil fuel-generating capacity for when there is not wind or sunlight.

This is one of the areas where the Department of Energy is able to make a specific contribution to Power Africa's capability by providing some of the expertise of our laboratories in these arenas.

I think it is worth calling out that the pledges from private-sector partners to the Beyond the Grid initiative are pretty considerable. It is more than $1 billion over the coming 5 years.

So while we don't have today specific, long lists of things that have gotten done, we think that this is a very promising area for the growth of Power Africa and in certain settings, there will be a lot of relevance.

Last comment: It is not just the village setting in rural Africa where off-grid and micro-grid systems are relevant, and that is equally true in remote settings in the United States, in Alaska, for example, and even in very nonrural settings, such as the micro-grids with separable grid systems, for example, that we are looking at in very, very highly urbanized parts of our country where, in times of grid instability, another commonality with some of the African grid systems, you can island off a particular part of the grid in order to protect critical load, hospitals, transport systems, et cetera.

Ms. BASS. Thank you.

I am sorry. Go ahead.

Mr. ICHORD. If I might, obviously, we know Africais blessed with world-class renewable energy resources. The U.S. is a member of the International Renewable Energy Agency, and what IRENA has been doing is to try to develop more extensive maps of the resource—renewable resource potential throughout Africa.

This is clearly showing that, in a sense, there is a range of resources, whether it is geothermal in Ethiopia, whether it is wind in Kenya, or hydro resources which are still very important for the continent and, in some cases, even solar power for larger grid-connected applications.

I was struck at the Africa ministerial in Addis about how consistent the ministers were in stressing the important role that they saw renewables playing in a diversified energy mix.

I don't know if you were, John.

And so I think that many countries have moved—they have moved to develop the incentive frameworks for interconnection of renewable energy. I think, in some cases, it—clearly they are looking at a mix of both renewables and natural gas to have cleaner fuel systems, and I think that varies widely, depending on whether you are talking about north or south or central.

Ms. BASS. Thank you.

Mr. WEBER [presiding]. Thank you.

You said in your opening remarks that you went to a meeting where there was about 500 participants, and I was just coming in and trying to get situated.

Where was that?

Mr. ELKIND. Thank you for the question.

This was the U.S.-Africa Energy Ministerial, which took place in early June in Addis Ababa, Ethiopia. It was hosted by the Government of Ethiopia, co-chaired by the Secretary of Energy, Dr. Moniz, and the Ethiopian Minister of Water, Irrigation, and Energy.

45

Mr. Weber. Okay. And then Mr. Postel, you said that Nigeria recently had privatized five generation companies and ten distribution companies. Is that correct?

Mr. Postel. Correct.

Mr. Weber. How long ago was that?

Mr. Postel. Over the course of the last 12 months.

Mr. Weber. Over the course of the last 12 months.

So the Government itself had been running on their generation and distribution facilities?

Mr. Postel. Yes, they had.

Mr. Weber. What percentage does that equate to in Nigeria? When you say they privatized five and ten, is that half of the facilities? A third?

Mr. Postel. I can get you the precise answer. Off the top of my head, I believe it was at least half, if not a bit more.

Mr. Weber. Okay. So in 12 months, has that been a viable function? Are they functioning properly with a little—I mean, I own a business. So it is impossible to do it without any problems. So he is grinning like a possum eating yellow jackets. So what does that mean? Are they operating without problems?

Mr. Postel. My colleague, Dr. Ichord, has some more recent information that he will add.

But my understanding is that each company is in a different situation in the sense that some are operating very well, some a few hiccups. But I would characterize them as growing pains. But, in general, a lot of the operations went forward, but——

Mr. Weber. Okay. And, by the way, I do want to add for our ranking member that Texas has its own grid. So you come to Texas, 85 percent of the State is covered by ERCOT. You are probably aware of that. If you want to know how to get that grid in Africa, come see us.

Next question—you are stuck on the possum eating the yellow jackets, huh?

Mr. Postel, from my notebook—notes about you, you said you had developed a plan to—first, international securitization of future receivables without a corporate guarantee.

Mr. Postel. Yes, sir.

Mr. Weber. Explain that.

Mr. Postel. This was a financing for the Government of Jamaica in 1988. It was the first new funding that they had obtained from the private sector in something like 13 years because there had been re-schedulings.

And, basically, every year they were receiving payments from AT&T for telephone calls that the Diaspora was making to Jamaica, and we felt that that was predictable enough to give them the money up front, in essence. And so we raised money in Japan and we did that financing, and it was all repaid.

Mr. Weber. And can you do the same thing with electrification in Africa?

Mr. Postel. I will have to think about that. I don't know.

Mr. Weber. Okay. That is what I thought it was.

Dr. Ichord, I think you also said in your remarks governance and transparency were key security concerns, protection of the people and the environment from sector impacts. It should be—I think I was writing fast and furiously, although that is a bad term now, isn't it? I was writing quickly.

What does that mean, ''sector impacts''?

Mr. ICHORD. Well, I think, obviously, the—as we know from our experience here, the environmental impact of offshore and upstream oil and gas is a very important area to develop the capacity of these countries, and that is really what it was in that context.

Maybe the ''sector impacts'' is a little too vague, but that is what we were talking about, increasing the capacities in the environmental management area.

Mr. WEBER. That is what I was wondering.

And then you also said something about EITI, the extractive——

Mr. ICHORD. Yeah. It is an international initiative, the Extractive Industries Transparency Initiative. Actually, the U.S. is participating. We are a candidate now. The Interior Department in the U.S. has the lead on it, and it is basically to enhance accountability in terms of this important sector and the revenues.

Mr. WEBER. Okay. That is going to be important.

You said, also, that—and I don't remember if you said Africa or a particular country was at a crossroads—I think Africa—they had expansive renewable resources and emerging oil and gas market—or, I guess, resources.

Mr. ICHORD. Right.

Mr. WEBER. Quantify that for us percentage-wise. Fifty-fifty? Sixty-forty?

Mr. ICHORD. Well, I think that clearly there are a dozen or more countries where oil and gas is developing. Some are more developed, like Angola and Nigeria. Others, where exploration is just beginning and in the early stages. I think it is a little bit too early to say exactly what that mix will be.

You have—certainly have countries like Tanzania and Mozambique where you have world-scale gas resources that are being developed, and that will then open up lots of opportunities for them to have a significant gas role in their economics.

At the same time, for the electric power sector, the economics of many of these renewable energy resources look very attractive, especially compared to oil, which many of the countries are still—you know, are having to use oil to generate and have a cost of, you know, 30 cents a kilowatt hour for power, like in Ghana, which has to use oil because they are not able to get gas from Nigeria in the pipeline.

Mr. WEBER. So I looked at a map of Africa, doing a search for pipeline infrastructure, and it looks like what limited pipeline infrastructure they have is primarily in the north. I don't know if you are familiar with that map or not.

Mr. ICHORD. Well, you have the west Africa pipeline, and that is——

Mr. WEBER. Runs from Algeria to Nigeria?

Mr. ICHORD. The pipeline is only in west Africa and does not reach Algeria.

Mr. WEBER. Okay.

Mr. ICHORD. So the problem has been that Nigeria has a severe gas shortage because the internal policies haven't given the incentives for the development of their gas resources. And, therefore, countries like Ghana and others on the pipeline route have not been able to get the gas supplies through that pipeline.

Mr. WEBER. Is there a robust pipeline industry and/or association in Africa that is pushing for the installation of pipelines? And do we have property rights? And how does that play if there is?

Mr. ELKIND. Thank you, Congressman Weber.

There is, I think, a natural unavoidable tension that will have to play out here and that, frankly, was one of the really core elements of our discussion in June at the ministerial meeting that I just referred to in response to your question.

And that is, as one sees development of the oil and gas resources, particularly in some of the frontier provinces, east Africa in particular, how much of that is for domestic consumption versus export?

And, I mean, the international oil companies want to meet demand in the countries where they operate because that has a multiplier effect that is very, very beneficial for many of those companies, but they also need predictability in terms of off-take arrangements.

So, to your question of if there is a robust existing vision, I would say no. There is a great deal of interest and some fairly elaborated, some fairly ambitious ideas, goals, in terms of development of east African gas pipelines, for example, to take gas to power generation in South Africa from Mozambique, as one—and Tanzania—one big example.

But the open issue, which still has not yet played out, is whether the steps can be put in place, the right policies, the right laws, that give the investors enough predictability so that they will put down, tens and tens of billions of dollars for really multi-decade investment——

Mr. WEBER. Well, and that brings me to—well, I have got a question about ranking of the most favorable countries, because clearly some countries are going to be better candidates than others on investing into infrastructure.

But before I go there, Mr. Elkind, you also said that you all had a focus on performance of products in the marketplace, making sure off-grid systems actually perform.

Now, when you say an "off-grid system," describe one of those to us.

Mr. ELKIND. Yes, sir.

So a small household or village-level system that might include one or more solar panels, perhaps paired with either storage capacity, battery systems or a fossil fuel—a diesel or other fossil fuel-generating system to use when the sun is not up, the wind is not blowing. That through to highly efficient lamps, refrigeration for food and medicine. Those kind of applications.

Mr. WEBER. So is that to say that, if someone has a house out there with solar panels, there is going to be an effort to have regulatory rules in place that they have to meet certain efficiency requirements?

Mr. ELKIND. No, sir. The point here is that there are lots of examples that one can see, for example, in solar lanterns where are products that are being sold into a number of marketplaces, including a number of the African countries, where the claims for the performance of the product simply don't match what the product actually does. You know, in our context, we call that false advertising.

And so, when the countries are saying, "How do we think about the technical challenge of knowing what product actually does what it says?," that is an area where we have experience in the United States and can help to make that experience available. Again, it is at their request and the point is not to allow fraudulent claims in the marketplace.

Mr. WEBER. Well, the last thing—and I don't mean to speak for you. But, apparently, one of the things you could say is the last thing you want to happen is, as they are developing these markets, they get burned with bad products and they just say, "They don't work. Forget it. Never mind."

All right. Now, is there any—and I don't know—I guess all three of you all. This is my last question that I alluded to earlier.

A ranking of the most favorable countries. I mean, I am going to have to believe—and you all have done a lot of thought on this. I haven't. But just at a glance, there is going to be a lot of factors that are going to influence whether they are a good candidate: Population, topography, gas/oil pipeline availability, educational resources. Do you have that work for us that you can come in there and you can train how to do this?

And then, of course, I mentioned earlier property ownership. Can you own property? Is there a system in place to take over, to condemn property, if you will, for pipeline, a right-of-way? The timing. Is it right for the country? Stability. Is it a stable system of government?

So those are just seven things I came up with. Do you rank countries, which would be the best candidates for investment in their infrastructure?

Mr. POSTEL. Congressman, thank you for your question. And it sounds like you were at some of these meetings where these kinds of things were discussed by listing all of those criteria——

Mr. WEBER. No. The NSA was there. I just got the tapes. I am sorry.

Mr. POSTEL. So we don't have a public listing, per se. But in the first phase of Power Africa, we did very carefully, through a rigorous interagency process, discuss which would be the six focus countries. And the factors that you describe are indeed many of the things that we looked at to try to assess who would be the good partners, and we will go through a similar process as we think about the expansion.

There is plenty to say on all of them. But one of the ones that I will just spend a moment on is the host country's commitment. Because as some of the other testimony alluded to, if you are trying to have viable electric utilities, if you are trying to solve some of problems that our private-sector investors have encountered in trying to do viable deals, you have got to have a commitment to do things differently.

And so that was one of the many components, but that was one of the most important components, to make sure that we really had committed partners who would do this in partnership with us and the private sector.

Mr. ICHORD. Well, Congressman, I can't give you a ranking. But, obviously, I mentioned a number of the countries that we are working with on the oil and gas side that at different stages in their development. Some are more gas-prone. Others look like they, you know, have good oil potential, like Angola, et cetera.

I think the companies are—you know, we have a range of companies, and U.S. included, that are working in these areas and that they are assessing the risk and they are assessing the commercial viability of these resources. There is a lot of exploratory drilling that is planned in some of these countries.

So we will have—I think—a lot of activity in this area. So I think it is going to be a couple years before this sort of shakes out in terms of where are the biggest opportunities.

But clearly Mozambique and Tanzania, in terms of the world-scale gas resources, are ones that everyone is looking at, both for export as well as for looking at the potential for east Africa and the whole—and including, in South Africa, the potential for that gas to have and develop the infrastructure.

There was recently a seminar that we had as part of the ministerial that looked at the east Africa gas infrastructure opportunities. That was done by the Columbia Energy Center that there is a report on that I would be happy to send you on that issue.

I think, on terms of the issue of the investment climate, the question of whether countries are, whether investors are willing to come in without sovereign guarantees is a key factor.

And in some countries, I think, you know, investors are saying, "Well, in Kenya, we can do that. We are willing to come in without a sovereign guarantee." In other countries, you won't.

So you then have to look to: Are there partial risk guarantees and other mechanisms that the World Bank or others can put in place that will mitigate some of the risk of the investment?

Mr. WEBER. Okay. Thank you. That answers my questions.

I recognize Mr. Stockman.

Mr. STOCKMAN. I thank you for the panel to come out today, on a Friday.

And, Dr. Ichord, according to your testimony, you have been in government for 40 years and you mentioned you were in Bangladesh. So was that a good 40 years or so ago.

My question is: When I was over there in Nigeria, they were mentioning some policies. And I am wondering—you had standards—are there any standards which prevent interaction by the State Department which is predicated on the Government's social policies or is it a strictly benign interpretation of their capabilities?

In other words, when I was in Nigeria, they were trying to free the girls that were kidnapped, and the U.S. military said, "We need to get permission from our Government to give them and facilitate information," and it was denied because of the interpretation of the present leadership in Nigeria.

I am wondering: Do you have similar restrictions on governments such as Uganda and Nigeria and saying, "We don't get involved because of their social policies" or is that a separate issue?

Mr. ICHORD. Well, I think, as we look at our overall engagement in the countries, we will work very closely with the Ambassador and the Embassy in assessing the political situation, the severity of the issues, if there are social or human rights issues, and make a decision on a case-by-case basis.

I think it is hard to generalize other than to say that, in a sense, we are not just sort of pursuing energy for energy's sake. I mean, it is part of our broader foreign policy interest in that it takes into account a lot of these questions.

Mr. STOCKMAN. Could you get me—or maybe you know off the top of your head, is Nigeria or Uganda—are there restrictions that you have in terms of working with them on energy?

Mr. ICHORD. I think right now—we started in Uganda early on in terms of the Energy Governance and Capacity Initiative, and we have done a lot of work on the geophysical side, environmental, land use planning, et cetera. I think the situation now, to the best of my understanding, is that we have put on hold any further work in Uganda.

Mr. STOCKMAN. And that is because of the social policies?

Mr. ICHORD. So I was informed that we have scaled back our activities. We are looking at whether we can proceed now. So it is——

Mr. STOCKMAN. But I was asking: Is that because of social policies that you scaled back?

Mr. ICHORD. I think it was a combination of things, but I would have to get back to you on the specifics.

Mr. STOCKMAN. I was going to say I would appreciate that. I think that would be very helpful. I think, actually, Congressman Smith would be interested in that and so I think would Congressman Weber. I think we would all be interested in that.

I have to tell you, on a personal level, when I was in Nigeria—and I think it actually was from—I think Mr. Postel's department who advocated that we not involve our military intelligence in helping Nigeria because of some of the interpretations of the current Government's positions.

To me, that was a little bit alarming because I now found out today that the Chinese have given Nigeria some of the equipment that they have been requesting from the United States, and my fear is, because of our policies, that we may be driving—as you know, the continent is really being recolonized not by the British, not by the Americans, but by the Chinese.

I mean, in the Republic of Congo and the DRC, there is a whole mountain of copper, as you know, that was sold for pennies on the dollar and the Chinese have their workers there and there is no kind of interplay or development with the host country.

It is very much—in fact, I would argue worse than what the colonial governments ever did and, yet, the Chinese are continually expanding their breadth of involvement. And my concern is that we are putting restrictions on ourselves to the degree that now we have become less important to those host countries.

So as you go forward, I would hope that you would see that the Chinese are a serious player and that in terms of competing with the United States, could be very problematic down the line.

Mr. Postel, you are shaking your head yes. So I hope you can tell me.

Mr. POSTEL. Thank you, Congressman.

I will definitely take note of your comments, and I will investigate further in discussion with the head of our office there. I am not familiar with all the circumstances of this, but certainly fully recognize the point you are making about the very active presence of China in Africa.

Mr. STOCKMAN. Yes. And I just say I think sometimes we should do more pragmatic analysis and not involve so much the—I mean, we need to balance it, I guess, in order to compete with our Chinese competitors. And it is—almost every country, whether it is Chad or Egypt or sub-Saharan Africa, I keep seeing the Chinese in a heavy, heavy way.

And, privately, I think it was the Republic of Congo. Some of the administrators said they prefer Americans, but the hurdles—well, and for reasons in past history, they have—some of those countries have embezzled and taken a lot of money from their own people.

So, in some way, it is justified. But my more concern is the interpreting of internal social policies, I think, are beyond the scope of what I think the United States should be doing. And I just want to express that.

And, also, I think, in terms of the oil development, and particularly in sub-Saharan Africa, there are companies in my district, Baker Hughes and Halliburton. So I guess Halliburton now technically is in Abu Dhabi, but—or Dubai. It kind of moved.

They would like to be in there, but there is, as you know, the Foreign Corrupt Practices Act, and there can be some misinterpretation of that law being applied to our own companies. And to that extent, I think there is a great deal of frustration on our side in Houston where we would like to see more cooperation.

And I think, in deference to our own corporations, if you could give them guidance and what they can do to facilitate more of involvement in those countries would be a great boon—well, Texas is already booming. We have no problem with fracking in our state. But I am still saying I think it would be beneficial to the United States, and maintaining that would keep our influence there.

But I am just alarmed at the rise—and you guys know I am right—about the rise of China in there. And it is obvious they have almost no restrictions whatsoever and they have no compunction about paying leaders large sums of money in order to facilitate their advantages.

And, with that, I yield back to my chairman now.

Mr. SMITH [presiding]. Thank you very much.

Before we go to the second panel, I would just like to ask one final question, and it has to do with—you know, obviously, the terrorist threats to many countries and people in Africa from Boko Haram to al-Shabaab are very significant.

And I am wondering how Power Africa integrates protecting the infrastructure and, of course, the people, the personnel, against terrorist attack, including cyber attacks, which we know could be devastating to an electrical power-generating grid or any other that is out there. So if you could perhaps speak to that issue, protecting and hardening it to terrorism.

Mr. ELKIND. Thank you for the question, Chairman Smith.

I will defer to my colleagues specifically in relation to Power Africa and those engagements there.

I can tell you that the recognition that we encounter from energy companies and energy agencies, ministries, in our international engagements to an ever-increasing degree recognize the importance of protecting infrastructure.

One of the things that the Department of Energy does is to enter into cooperative engagements with key international partners, and we do this at their expense, at the expense of the host country, to help them identify vulnerabilities, plan their systems, so that they are resilient to any threat.

It is an all-hazard approach, whether one is talking about severe weather, cyber attack, or physical attack and we have found that this is an area where the United States is in a position to add a tremendous amount of value from our experience.

I will have to defer to my colleagues as to whether that is being done in the Power Africa case. I simply don't know the answer myself.

Mr. POSTEL. Thank you for the question, Mr. Chairman.

I will double-check, but I believe that some of these exchanges, depending on the topics that are of interest to the energy regulators, the power pool operators or the utilities, I believe some of these exchanges that I will be sending you details of have included those kinds of topics.

The other important thing is just the involvement of the private sector because a lot of the private-sector investors have a lot of experience in thinking through these risks and, when they are investing from offshore, I think, they are looking at all risk.

And that is another avenue in on this topic, which is they stand to lose a lot of money if they don't pay attention to these topics. And so we also count on them to be very involved, working with local folks, to look at that.

Mr. SMITH. But just to be certain, it is not an afterthought. It is integrated into planning, development, and the like, and as well as implementation?

Mr. POSTEL. I want to double-check on that, sir, because I don't know if it has been always demand-driven or whether it is integrated to, also. I will come back to you with specifics.

Mr. SMITH. I appreciate that. Thank you.

Mr. ICHORD. I would just say that we are in the early stage of really developing the electricity grid systems in Africa. We have the three power pools—east, west, and south—at their different stages.

I think that, in that process and working with the international financial institutions like the World Bank and African Development Bank, I mean, there is a lot of consideration about the security and reliability issues that are going into the development of the loan programs and specifications for what kind of systems they can put in place.

But clearly it is going to be an issue that is going to be with us, especially as they begin to invest more and more in developing high-voltage transmissions systems.

Mr. SMITH. Now, would the expertise of Homeland Security, the Pentagon, or State Department's Diplomatic Security be incorporated?

I say that because, after we got hit in Dar es Salaam and in Nairobi, I chaired the hearings for the Accountability Review Board after the 1998 terrorist attack, and I will never forget when Assistant Secretary Carpenter said that they will look for any vulnerability, that nothing is off limits. I am paraphrasing, of course. But he sat right where you sat in 1999 when I chaired the hearings.

And out of that I wrote the Embassy Security Act, which became law, and it added much, the setbacks that Bobby Inman had talked about were all finally implemented because they had not been implemented for years. And they are still in the process, of course, in some of our missions abroad.

But it was a lesson I learned, you know, that people just thought it wouldn't happen here and, you know, let the guard down. And, of course, you know, those who wish us ill, these nefarious networks, will look for any vulnerability, to use your word, which I think is the right word.

If you could get back to us, if you would, how that whole process of protecting—and I am glad you elaborated as well that it is not just against terrorism, but it is against earthquakes and natural disasters as well, if the subcommittee in any way could be helpful, even in promoting more of that.

Because I think, going forward, they will be increasingly at risk. I mean, the terrorists are not foolish. They will look for anything which will do maximum damage. So if you could get back. But I thank you for your answers as well.

Ms. Bass, anything?

Ms. BASS. No.

Mr. SMITH. Anything you would like to say before we conclude?

Mr. POSTEL. Well, I think I could speak on behalf of my colleagues both at the table and in our agencies that we just reiterate our thanks to all of you for your leadership and your interest. We are not going to collectively solve this challenge without your help, and we very much appreciate it.

Mr. SMITH. Well, thank you. It is a partnership. Thank you for taking the lead and doing it so effectively. The subcommittee, I know members on both sides of the aisle, are greatly appreciative of what you have accomplished and will accomplish going forward. Thank you.

I'd like to now welcome our second panel, beginning first with Mr. Walker Williams, who is president and CEO of Leadership Africa USA and Alternative Marketing Access.

Mr. Williams is a management consultant with more than 3 decades of experience working with governments, corporations, NGOs, and multilateral institutions. His areas of expertise and strategic advice include energy, infrastructure development, finance management, and communications. He has worked with the U.S. Department of Energy on the first U.S.-Africa Energy Ministerial in Morocco and another this past year in Ethiopia.

I just would note as well Mr. Williams was also instrumental in bringing the House and Senate together with the African Diplomatic Corps for an historic and now ongoing set of meetings that we have had to meet with the African Ambassadors and DCMs and others from all of the African countries.

And I want to thank you for your leadership in making that happen.

We then will hear from Ms. Dianne Sutherland, who has been working within Africa for the past 17 years, 13 of those years as a resident of Egypt.

Ms. Sutherland entered the oil and gas publishing business in 2001 and, by late 2002, launched what is known as Petroleum Africa magazine. In January 2008, she also launched Alternative Energy Africa magazine. Additionally, Ms. Sutherland offers her services as consultant to Resource Development Financial Consultants of Ghana.

We will be hooking up with her by way of video.

But, if you would, Mr. Williams, begin with your testimony.

## STATEMENT OF MR. WALKER A. WILLIAMS, PRESIDENT AND CHIEF EXECUTIVE OFFICER, LEADERSHIP AFRICA USA

Mr. WILLIAMS. Thank you, Chairman Smith, Ranking Member Bass, Member Stockman. I appreciate greatly this opportunity to come before you this afternoon to talk about energy.

It is something that is of critical importance not only to Africa, it is important to the U.S. economy. And I have got some prepared remarks I am going to refer to, and I have also submitted testimony.

I am going to take a different take than our first panel because I am coming from the civil society side of the ledger. And I wanted to take a few moments and talk about Leadership Africa.

We do programs throughout Africa and, before that, I was very instrumental in working in the Caribbean on the Caribbean Basin Initiative and we worked on AGOA. And I want to say to you any NGO or civil society organization working in Africa can only implement programs if there is energy and power and electricity.

I mean, we are kidding ourselves. My emphasis has always been on education and, if we don't have electricity in the schools or we don't have computers, the kids aren't getting an education. So, by necessity, we have adopted and started to work and move into the energy sector in order to ensure that the programs that we put together can be leveraged and can be sustainable.

Now, Chairman Smith referred to some meetings that we did several years ago, but the little background on that was the African Ambassadors group and they meet regularly, once a month, but they were not involved in the deliberations around AGOA.

So 2, 3 years ago we took it upon ourselves to start meeting with them informally. And we wanted to hear from the African Ambassadors, we wanted to hear from the beneficiaries of these programs that we talked about earlier this morning, what their take was, what thoughts they had about solutions to some of the challenges that are affecting them and that they are confronting. And with that in mind, we spent some time working on AGOA.

Now, AGOA is up for reauthorization between now and September 15th, and it is a very important initiative. But I am going to say here this afternoon that we, as the NGO community, we, as civil society—we link AGOA to energy.

If you don't have energy, you are not going to make the kinds of changes and have the kind of productivity that you want through AGOA because you can't industrialize. You don't have the energy and the power to meet the metrics and solve the solution.

So I am saying to you we link, like the African Ambassadors link and like the heads did at the leaders' summit—they link AGOA and they link energy. They are two key, key priorities for them.

I want to suggest that, when I mention in my prepared remarks references to AGOA, it is because they see AGOA linked to energy. We don't do it quite that way, but that is how the African Ambassadors and that is how the African heads look at those two issues.

There was reference earlier this morning to the U.S.-Africa Energy Ministerial. Well, Leadership Africa had the privilege of coordinating that meeting in Ethiopia on behalf of U.S. Department of Energy. So I was happy to hear that the U.S. Department of Energy and those who attended thought it was successful.

And, yes, we did have 500 participants. We had about 120 corporations, both U.S. and African companies, participate, and it was successful enough that, when I came back, and what I had heard in Ethiopia, I have been pushing—and this is the point I want to make—that we need follow-up.

We need consistent, intentional follow-up. We didn't get into it to coordinate with the U.S. Department of Energy—and we had 13 U.S. agencies participating—without there being follow-up. The focus of that was Power Africa. They announced Beyond the Grid at that session in Ethiopia, and it is going forward.

But I am going to suggest and pick up on what Ranking Member Bass said earlier, that we also need to bring additional players to the table. And in my prepared remarks, I talk about small, minority, and women-owned businesses, and I talk about that in linking them with their counterparts in Africa.

Now, why do I say that? If you look at what is going on in the continent, there is a policy which the African governments call "localization." They are saying to our U.S. companies that, "If you really want to work in our country and if you are looking for business opportunities in our country, you need to find a way to train our local citizens. You need to find a way to participate."

So it is in our self-interest, and I think there is a nice marriage between our small business community and the African business community to share, to twin, to work together around and under Power Africa and, of course, MCC's program because there is a—what we would refer to in the private sector, a money sock. And where there is money, you know you are going to get paid.

Then we just need to make sure that these programs encourage those companies, our U.S. companies and others, reaching out to their smaller business communities to make sure there are opportunities for them to participate.

I also in my prepared remarks talk about something that I think needs to be more focused on, and that is what I called regionalization. I believe and I have put forward and made suggestions that the way to really deal effectively with energy, electricity, and power is on a regional strategy, working with the regional groupings that are already in place in Africa. Because, in some sense, you might find it is easier to take electricity from Ghana and ship it into a neighboring country than it is to use it internally.

So I have urged—I have been in conversations with DOE, and I think that is a strategy that, if they can find a way to do that, it starts to lead to some other things which we call trade facilitation. See, electricity is so powerful that, if you came to me and said that, "We are going to have a regional approach on electricity," it starts to get to trade facilitation among the leaders because it is something that they all share a need for. You just get them talking and you start to break down some of the barriers around working across borders and—in terms of these priorities.

I didn't, as you notice, repeat the statistics. We know that over 600 million people in Africa are without electricity. We know that Africa needs resources. But the other thing that Africa does need, it needs training in capacity development, and that is something that the U.S. Government and our agencies are very capable of providing and doing.

We just need to make sure that they continue to work together like they are doing with the Power Africa working group, which is an excellent program. I am pushing very hard for the EAA program, the Electrify Africa program, because it sort of stabilizes and puts in place a long-term solution.

And I am also saying that we need to encourage and listen to our African partners. We need to hear from them and we need to look at more partnering relationships to maintain our competitive advantage.

You know, when the agencies talk—and I am a little bit involved in the industry—the agencies don't control any energy. You know, they don't control any oil. And so you really do need to find a way to create public-private partnerships and be supportive of those entities in the U.S. that do have access to these resources and hear from them like I am listening to the African Ambassadors and the African heads on what they think will help them do a better job and create employment opportunities not only here in the U.S., but in Africa.

And I think, with that, I will defer to my other counterpart, if she is here.

[The prepared statement of Mr. Williams follows:]

**Statement of**
Walker A. Williams
President & CEO
Leadership Africa USA

**Before the**
House Committee on Foreign Affairs
The Future of Energy in Africa
November 14, 2014

Thank you Chairman Smith, Ranking Member Bass, and Members of the Committee; I appreciate the opportunity to be here today to discuss Leadership Africa USA's efforts to promote energy security in Africa.

As President and CEO of Leadership Africa USA (LA USA), with over three decades of experience working with NGOs and multilateral institutions, I have provided strategic counsel on energy, infrastructure development, finance, management and communications.

Under my leadership, Leadership Africa USA (LA USA) is working with the African Ambassadors Group and their AGOA Working Committee through congressional briefings and meetings with members of Congress, around energy, leadership, education, training, and economic development.

Previously, I advised the government of Trinidad & Tobago's consultants on several regional Energy Ministerials for CARICOM countries and for the 'Summit of the Americas' which was attended by U.S. President Barack Obama.

I also worked with DOE on their first U.S.-Africa Energy Ministerial in Morocco and this past June assisted the U.S. Department of Energy and the governments of Ethiopia and the United States to co-host a historic U.S.-Africa Energy Ministerial (AEM) in Addis Ababa, Ethiopia --- 'Catalyzing Sustainable Energy Growth in Africa'. This AEM focused on the need for increased investment in Africa's electricity and energy sectors was attended by energy and power ministers from over 40 African countries, over 130 U.S. and African businesses, and a U.S. Government Delegation led by Energy Secretary Moniz that included EXIM Bank, USAID, OPIC, USTDA, MCC, the State Department and Administration officials. I am currently finalizing plans to operate the first gas-to-liquid (GTL) plant in the Western Hemisphere.

Africa is the new frontier for development with increasing opportunities for the United States and the private sector to align our interests to take advantage of this paradigm shift. However, the lack of electricity and energy are major challenges impeding Africa's economic growth and investments.

Africa's development agenda is accelerating and U.S. policies towards Africa's growth need to be more robust and better coordinated in a resource hungry world. Since September 11, 2001, and the dramatic changes in the Middle East and in North Africa have forever changed the African continent and increased the world's economic and political vulnerability. The fluid nature of these events has implications for U.S. policy in Africa and will impact Africa's democratic trajectory.

Sub-Saharan Africa is a region of great strategic importance and vast natural resources with new resource discoveries expected for years to come. Today, Africa is open for business and America needs to stay engaged in Africa. Africa supplies almost 25% of U.S. oil imports and exports are expected to rise with fossil fuels continuing to be the main U.S. driver and energy resource for many decades to come.

Most energy economists believe Africa's gas and oil resources (Gulf of Guinea, The Maghreb, and Central Africa, etc) will over the next decade continue to expand. African energy producing countries --- Ghana, Sao Tome and Principe, Guinea, Nigeria, Democratic Republic of the Congo, Gabon, Angola, Cameroon, Chad, The Republic of the Congo, Equatorial Guinea, and the Sudan all rely on their energy reserves for their countries economic growth and income but at levels significantly below their countries needs or growth potential leading to economic distortions that historically have stymied development and accelerated instability.

When President Obama visited Ghana in 2009, he acknowledged that Africa's growth and stability contributes to our own growth and for Africa's sustainable development and growth energy is a key driver. The United States continuing economic development and national security interests in a global economy require dependable access to secure and sustainable energy supplies and the formulation for a more comprehensive and competitive U.S. energy strategy to stay competitively engaged in Africa.

Endowed with vast natural resources Africa is attracting global attention and needs committed partners to assist these resource rich African countries obtain their rightful places in the global economy.

Few issues pose greater challenge to Africa's sustainable development and democratic gains than natural resource management and development especially among African countries experiencing recent energy discoveries who have neither the laws, experience nor the institutional capacity to govern this sector. Africa's sustainable development agenda is at a crossroad and with beneficial support and committed partners the 21st Century should be Africa's century to grow.

The U.S. has an excellent opportunity to assist Africa overcome challenges within their energy and natural resource sectors and advance our national and global energy security interest. Now is not the time to turn inward or to retreat from Africa.

Our current U.S. energy strategy toward Africa needs better focus and coordination to achieve actionable policies and strategies. America faces a choice – we are in a global energy race but need to be more focused, strategic, and not on the sidelines.

Overcoming growing U.S. interdependence on energy will require partnering, collaboration and creative thinking to address the many risks and challenges facing U.S. energy companies, stakeholders and investors interested in doing business in Africa.

A renewed U.S. business and government posture should involve the creation of new energy-related partnerships (building bridges), constructive engagements and beneficial policy initiatives that showcase the U.S. Government's commitment and responsiveness to Africa's energy priorities. Government statements of good intentions toward Africa should be matched with the implementation of meaningful policy changes and initiatives with strategies that are compatible with the following African development pillars:

- Sustainable Peace
- Human Rights
- Capacity Development
- Economic Empowerment

With tensions in the Middle East on the rise and relations with Russia, the Ukraine, and Iran, and similar emerging global hotspots unfolding the U.S. Government's efforts to strengthen Africa's democratic institutions and promote good governance should be to increase on all fronts interactions with resource-rich African countries.

The U.S. Government's ability to reshape U.S. energy policy towards Africa with limited agency and government resources is an outdated strategy that should be revised to be more supportive of U.S. interest in Africa. This goal to increase financing and to remove political hurdles for U.S. investors needs to be a top government priority.

Africa, according to the International Energy Agency's (IEA) economist Dr. Birol in the last 5 years over 25 percent of global oil discoveries were in sub-Saharan Africa where 620 million people, almost two-thirds of the population lived without electricity. IEA estimates that by 2040 without meaningful strategic investments in Africa's power sector over 500 million people in rural communities will still not have power. Renewables, like solar, hydro, and wind are an untapped potential that need to be more fully explored to provide access to energy throughout Sub-Saharan Africa.

The IEA's prediction that sub-Saharan Africa will be a major natural gas producer in 2014 and U.S. production of shale gas will over time exceed Russia's gas production, which is already pushing Europe to develop policies and initiatives that support the development of Africa's energy resources. Sub-Saharan Africa will be a cornerstone of global oil markets and an emerging gas supplier for Europe in the future.

New approaches are needed to address poverty in Africa by the government and the U.S. private sector and Leadership Africa USA sees energy as key to successful poverty reduction strategies in Africa.

Africa is the lowest recipient of global investment resources as compared with other regions in the world. Africa receives less than 1% of American investments worldwide. Africa's bid for enhanced domestic and foreign investments flows will not yield positive results if sustainable solutions are not found to address factors inhibiting Africa's growth. In addition to access to energy resources, other inhibiting factors include technology, inadequate infrastructure, capacity development, lack of political stability, limited national markets, image issues and Africa's investment climate. Infrastructural challenges in Africa are daunting to provide stable power and access to electricity. Africa needs massive investment to be instrumental in facing their development challenges.

Africa currently has a 70 percent energy deficit and in response to this deficit, the Administration launched their Power Africa Initiative, committing public and private sector funding focused on renewable energy across six African countries. The U.S. Department of Energy, in support of Power Africa, reached out to African Energy and Power Ministers and the U.S. private sector to reinforce the U.S. government's support to improve Africa's access to a mix of energy resources which launched the U.S.-Africa Energy Ministerial.

Leadership Africa USA was pleased to be a part of the U.S.-Africa Energy Ministerial (AEM). The agenda and goals of the Ministerial, which highlighted energy as a key economic driver for Africa's development, align neatly with our organization's international development programs and focus on Africa's youth.

Our goal is to ensure Africa's development future and assist African youth escape poverty, and excel to become the leaders of the future. To fulfill our goal to provide Africa's youth the opportunities to develop the necessary skills they need to be productive stakeholders of their societies, the benefits of energy and power have to be extended into their communities.

It is our hope that the government-to-government, government-to-industry, and company-to-company exchanges on policy and investment that took place during this Energy Ministerial, will serve to increase cross-border power trade, improvements in the existing energy infrastructure, and increase access to electricity for Africa and its youth. We also believe it is important to support workforce development for these efforts to be sustainable.

Developing the energy and power sector in Africa will be a enormous undertaking and according to the International Energy Agency (IEA) will require over $300 billion in new investments to achieve universal electricity by 2030.

U.S. companies as we witnessed during the AEM and the recent U.S.-Africa Leaders Summit recognize they are dealing with a new Africa with profitable business opportunities for their companies and need our government policies and support to level the playing field in Africa.

As an NGO and based on our work with the African Ambassadors Group, our development initiatives are to always hear directly from the Africans themselves, their own solutions to the challenges they face. We always identify and work with local partners for sustainability with value chain strategies in place before we launch. Our recommendations for today's hearing center around globalization; the critical need for follow-up; partnerships; Africa's localization strategies and developing creative arrangements supporting the US private sector; regionalization; and bringing new players to the table including SMEs, civil society organizations, and better networking.

### *Small and Medium Enterprises (SMEs)*
Federal agencies should work to leverage synergies between the appropriate government programs with the potential to encourage more SME's participation as part of our energy policy. A concerted effort by DOE, the State Department, Commerce and other U.S. agencies to link this business community to meaningful commercial opportunities and joint ventures with African counterparts would be a very positive action to take in support of U.S. energy security and to help lessen China's advantage.

Africans and African Americans are linked by history and self-determination and the U.S. SME community's historic interest in Africa's development. American and African SMEs should be an integral part of any renewed energy strategy for Africa and should be more targeted by other U.S. government agencies as part of a more integrated U.S. energy strategy.

We need to significantly broaden business opportunities for SME's to partner with African SMEs since both business communities have a great deal to share with each other to leverage business, investment and trade opportunities.

More support and collaboration for SMEs to be more involved in Africa represents an underutilized resource and our challenge is to intentionally include this business community in a renewed U.S. African energy strategy.

The U.S. Government's mission must include advocacy on behalf of all U.S. businesses both large and small including SMEs to identify opportunities and assist them in navigating foreign regulations, handling disputes, investment opportunities and contracts.

Today's global marketplace is tough, competitive, fast changing and the stakes are high. To win today requires strategic clarity --- a clear vision, where we are today and where do we want to go tomorrow.

## AGOA

Leadership Africa USA began working with the African Ambassadors Group in November 2011 when we organized the *'First Ever Joint House and Senate* Briefing' with the Subcommittees on Africa and the African Diplomatic Corps. LA USA and the African Ambassadors Group's AGOA efforts have continued through the African Ambassadors Group, which have included Congressional-Diplomatic Dialogue, Congressional Conversations, briefings, meetings, events, and outreach that resulted in specific recommendations from the African Ambassadors for the reauthorization of AGOA.

It's our belief following the recent U.S-Africa Energy Ministerial (AEM) in Ethiopia and the U.S-Africa Leaders Summit that the U.S government is ready to focus on an African agenda, including reauthorization of AGOA, with a prevailing opinion supportive of AGOA's reauthorization.

In this context, the African Growth and Opportunity Act (AGOA), the cornerstone of the United States trade and investment policy towards sub-Saharan Africa, has made a positive impact on economic growth and job creation for both the U.S. and Africa since its enactment in 2000. It is estimated that AGOA has created 350,000 direct jobs and over 1,300,000 million indirect jobs in sub-Saharan Africa and over 100,000 jobs in the United States. AGOA has been the foundational initiative for expanding U.S-Africa trade since 2000 and both the Administration and Congress are focusing on AGOA's reauthorization including possible expansion.

### AFRICAN INPUT

The African Ambassadors provided LA USA a copy of their proposed agenda topics for the recent U.S. Africa Leaders Summit, a historic opportunity for the African Heads of State to engage in a comprehensive dialogue with United States officials, business leaders, and civil society organizations on ways to bolster trade and investment on both sides of the Atlantic.

Their talking points (and this is important) included their support for AGOA's reauthorization, which they tie directly to Africa's need for greater access to energy and power. Their recommendations and priorities which I have included, calling for AGOA's reauthorization and how important they would like AGOA's reauthorization to be linked to Africa's access to energy:

a. AGOA's renewal for a further 15 years with no-graduation of any country and the Third Country Fabric Provision should be made co-terminus;

b. The General System of Preferences (GSP) has expired and needs to be re-authorized;

c. Support for President Obama's Trade Africa Initiative and its contribution to boost intra-African trade;

d. Support for Africa's own strategic regional integration agenda to boost Africa's internal trade;

e. Significantly increased investments for infrastructural development to enhance economic growth and trade.

In support of Power Africa, the United States House of Representatives passed legislation "the Electrify Africa Act (EAA)."

The Electrify Africa Act of 2013 was introduced into the House of Representatives on June 27, 2013 by Representative Royce. The stated purpose is to "...improve access to affordable, reliable electricity in Africa in order to unlock the potential for economic growth, job creation, food security, improved health and education outcomes, and sustainable poverty reduction.

Compatible with Power Africa, the Electrify Africa Act (EAA), will establish a comprehensive U.S. Government policy to encourage an appropriate mix of power solutions, including renewable energy. EAA encourages U.S. government agencies support for the development of low-cost, base load energy resources with significant regional impact with minimal environmental damage. The "Electrify Africa Act" also identifies the provision of fast track power through the use of mobile aero-derivative dual-fuel turbines as a bridge to permanent installed capacity a strategy in the Bill that the US Government should support, promote and facilitate.

A key part of Power Africa's approach to the future of energy in Africa is leveraging the Millennium Challenge Corporation's (MCC) investments on the continent. MCC has already provided roughly $1 billion dollars in grants for power in Africa and is on track to provide another $1 billion to power to countries such as Ghana, Tanzania and Liberia.

Before the infrastructure needs are addressed through MCC's grants, MCC works with countries and private sector actors interested in also investing and requires willing countries to make the tough policy reforms needed to create a viable, sustainable sector.

This approach has proven successful when MCC's $498 million Ghana Power Compact was able to catalyze in excess of $4 billion of private sector commitment for the development of the energy sector.

These elements summarize our thinking on this legislation and support our views that in order to deliver on the promised results, the legislation should incorporate specific references to fast track bridging power through the use of dual fuel power plant with natural gas capability. The reference to fast track bridging power solution with natural gas capability addresses two essential elements— speed (fast-track bridging power) and low transmissions. This is the quickest way to achieve meaningful number in incremental installed MWs on the continent within a time frame that can be measured in weeks or months, not years.

The African Union on behalf of their members developed a Program for Infrastructure Development (PIDA) as part of 'horizon 2040' which outlines Africa's energy vision, including its intended energy mix and related power projects, such as the development of transmission corridors. The African Leaders are seeking support to ensure the harmonization and U.S. support to meet Africa's energy needs as articulated in PIDA.

a) Maintain on-going support for the Power Africa Initiative to reach the goal of producing 10 000 MW, and ensure that renewable energy continues to play a key role in Africa's energy mix;

b) Extend Power Africa's financial and geographic scope so that more countries and regional power pools benefit, in line with the Electrify Africa Act;

c) Solicit U.S. endorsement and support for the PIDA as the statement of Africa's energy needs, aspirations and plans, such as:

   i. The harnessing of Africa's hydro-electric power which has feasible potential of 1,750,000 GWh / year of which only 4.3% is currently exploited;

   ii. The promotion of 8 hydro-power projects, 4 transmission corridors, regional energy interconnection projects and 2 oil and gas pipelines up to 2020; and

   iii. A required investment of $43 billion annually to meet these targets.

d) The U.S. should also partner with Africa in enhancing its capacity to adapt to climate change as well as in meeting the continent's obligations to mitigate potential through the Power Africa Initiative, and through the transfer of Carbon Capture and Storage and other clean coal technologies to assist in the sustainable development of Africa's conventional energy resources;

e) The U.S. should support the acceleration of the exploration, harnessing, and benefaction of sources of unconventional energy resources in Africa, such as natural gas;

f) Encourage the hosting of a conference between Africa, the U.S. and multilateral agencies, involving public and private funds and investors, in order to highlight opportunities in the development of Africa's energy power projects and transmission corridors;

g) Commend the holding of the First U.S.-Africa Energy Ministerial Meeting that took place is Addis Ababa on June 3-4, 2014 and recommend the follow-up of discussions from the meeting and encourage the continuation of the U.S.-Africa Energy Ministerial Meeting.

To advance U.S. Government and business interest to support Africa's access to energy, Leadership Africa USA is proposing a regional approach to improve Africa's energy infrastructure to create new business opportunities for both African and U.S. companies.

REGIONALIZATION

The potential of intra-African regional trade is restricted and currently about 10%-12%, compared with North American trade with North American countries about 40%, and 63% by countries in Western Europe. The announced continental Free Trade Area by 2017 would, when established, expand Africa's integration and help to bring together fragmented African economies.

We recommend the Administration and Congress support outreach and efforts to Regional Economic Communities (RECs) as major points of contact as part of a regional public private partnerships (PPP) energy strategy. Africa's economic integration is the basis for any meaningful enhanced development in Africa. Energy security is a key building block if Africa is to achieve a sustainable future. REC's have great potential to support a U.S. Government and private sector-led regional energy strategy. Involving:

- Economic Community of West African States (ECOWAS)
- The Southern African Development Community (SADC)
- The African Union (AU)
- The East African Community (EAC)
- The Economic Community of Central African States (ECCAS)

**Why a regional energy strategy?**

- Promote regional ownership and support
- Discussions in planning followed by topical discussions on the follow-up themes on the AEM issues/meeting structure – purpose, composition of delegations, agenda, and venue.
- Focused regional meetings with flexible agenda for participants to express views for genuine dialogue and collaboration.
- High level political and private sector leadership through participation
- Technical experts
- Effective planning process on the way forward to achieve progress.
- A unified approach and collaboration to build consensus to achieve regional success.
- Advocacy and stewardship for Africa

We must mobilize to confront energy insecurity more in Africa and need a broad strategy and serious effort to work together. The U.S. must earn our place as Africa's trusted partner with U.S. business leadership in forefront. We believe the regional (PPP) energy strategy and approach Leadership Africa USA is proposing will contribute to:

- Regional policies and strategies toward regional energy security.
- Transcend regional competitions and embrace regional cooperation.
- Work with our Africa partners.
- Identify strengths and possibilities and then focus on leveraging those strengths to improve Africa's access to energy and power.
- More focused U.S. approach using the private sector technology and expertise to move beyond a government only solution.
- Public-private collaborations to unlock new funding, infrastructure, and development strategies.
- Small-Medium Enterprises (SMEs) include as part of the process going forward as a key part of any sustainable solution.

The U.S. has at times been slower to react to the new developments happening in Africa. But this dynamic is changing with Africa supplying more energy resources globally. Visionary African leaders understand the need to reform and improve key economic drivers such as education, infrastructure development, the rule of law, transportation, and capacity development to achieve sustained economic growth.

Energy impacts people's lives and expanding access to energy in sub-Saharan Africa will be an enormous African challenge. Africa needs electrification, and without increased electricity and access to power, Africa cannot grow. Many of these global energy and related issues present new challenges and opportunities for the United States and Africa that need to be addressed through committed leadership and new energy strategies.

Thank You

———————

67

Mr. SMITH. Mr. Williams, thank you very much for your testimony. Without objection, your full statement will be made a part of the record.

I would like to now welcome from Houston, Texas, Dianne Sutherland.

And you are recognized. Please proceed.

## STATEMENT OF MS. DIANNE R. SUTHERLAND, OWNER AND PUBLISHER, PETROLEUM AFRICA MAGAZINE

Ms. SUTHERLAND. I would like to extend my appreciation to the subcommittee for the invitation to testify at this hearing today on Africa's energy future.

Since entering the African energy industry over 14 years ago, I have witnessed a vast transformation in both the continent's fossil fuel and alternative energy sectors and, in parallel, significant growth in international investments.

Although Africa holds an abundance of fossil fuels and renewable energy resources, the continent is sorely underpowered in access to clean, affordable energy. It is a luxury to most of its over 1 billion population.

And despite the continent possessing 6 percent of global oil reserves and being responsible for about 10 percent of global production, the majority of Africans do not reap the benefits of their resources. Many of these underpowered countries earn incredible sums of revenue from their hydrocarbon, agricultural, and mining sectors, but very little is, in turn, invested into power infrastructure.

The companies opening up Africa's oil and gas potential are predominantly small- to mid-size independent firms with limited capital. They secure the exploration licenses, conduct the geophysical work, and then market their findings to larger multinational firms to secure funding and minimize their risk when it comes time to drilling.

This trend has been chiefly responsible for the major discoveries over the past 2 decades and the opening up of new frontier basins. In the past 10 years, significant oil and gas discoveries have been discovered in countries such as Ghana, Kenya, Mozambique, Tanzania, Uganda, and others.

Improved technology deployment has also played a large role in enabling these discoveries, with some of Africa's developments in the deep offshore rivaling that of those in the Gulf of Mexico.

And while natural gas was not too long ago considered a nuisance byproduct in sub-Saharan Africa, the resource is increasingly utilized in large-scale operations, such as LNG, power generation, trans-border pipelines, and also in smaller gas applications, such as LPG and CNG.

With the known natural gas reserves across north Africa and new discoveries in sub-Sahara, the continent is a natural gas player to be reckoned with in the future. In Mozambique and Tanzania alone, there is reasonable confidence that the two areas together hold a resource of at least 190 trillion cubic feet with expectations that proven reserves could more than double with future exploration.

And the shale boom is not exclusive to North America. Africa, too, has her share of unconventional resources. Shale oil, shale gas, and coal bed methane are all now receiving attention from both governments and the private sector, and a number of projects are afoot.

As for alternative energy, there are literally hundreds of small-scale projects established and in the works, not to mention the dozens of larger scale projects on the drawing board. These translate into billions of dollars of investment for the continent. The sector is making progress with new renewable-specific legislation emerging in many countries, facilitating development of the industry.

In addition to the major wind farm and solar projects online or under construction in Egypt, Ethiopia, Kenya, Morocco, and South Africa, the continent's hydropower resource is enormous, with some estimates having it accounting for 12 percent of the world's potential.

The Chinese are already heavily invested in Africa's hydropower and they are funding $500 million toward Cote d'Ivoire's Soubre Dam. Ethiopia is looking to develop 6 gigawatts of power with its Grand Renaissance Dam, and the Grand Inga scheme in the Democratic Republic of the Congo will be the world's largest if plans are implemented as envisioned.

Not to be left out is geothermal. Kenya is said to construct new geothermal power plants by December 2015, and, in fact, its strategy would make it the number one geothermal producer by the year 2033 if executed accordingly.

And having a near-term tangible impact on improving the lives of Africans are the many small-scale off-grid rural projects. These projects are varied and include household solar products, community waste, energy, rooftop solar and wind, and biofuel and biogas applications.

And perhaps the greatest achievement over the decade has been seen in the manufacturing sector with solar factories emerging to meet growing regional demand. This trend has lead to a technology transfer with Africans learning to provide services to their communities.

In addition, other small projects have allowed typical low-income villagers to become small business owners and, in turn, pass on technology to their communities. This development is certainly a success story for the continent by any measure.

And, in closing, the hydrocarbon and renewable initiatives set forth by African governments, as well as by their global partners, are paying huge dividends. While much progress has been made, there is a long road ahead to bring Africans up to a first world standard of living, and American know-how and investment can play a major role in making that happen.

Thank you.

[The prepared statement of Ms. Sutherland follows:]

**Dianne Sutherland**
**Owner & Publisher**
**Petroleum Africa & Alternative Energy Africa magazines**

**House Committee on Foreign Affairs,**
**Session: The Future of Energy in Africa**
**Date: November 14, 2014, 12 p.m.**

Since entering the African energy industry over 14 years ago, I have witnessed a vast transformation in both the continent's fossil fuel and alternative energy sectors and in parallel, significant growth in international investment.

Although Africa holds an abundance of both fossil fuels and renewable energy resources, the continent is sorely underpowered and access to clean, affordable energy is a luxury to most its over one billion population. Despite the continent possessing 6% of global oil reserves and being responsible for about 10% of global production, the majority of Africans do not reap the benefits of their resources. Many of these under-powered countries earn incredible sums of revenue from their hydrocarbon, agricultural and mining sectors but very little is in turn invested into power infrastructure.

The companies opening up Africa's oil and gas potential are predominantly small- to mid-size independent firms with limited capital. They secure the exploration licenses, conduct the geophysical work, and then market their findings to larger multi-national firms to secure funding and minimize their risk when it comes time to drill. This trend has been chiefly responsible for the major discoveries over the past two decades and the opening up of new frontier basins. In the past 10 years, significant oil and gas reserves have been added in countries such as Ghana, Kenya, Mozambique, Tanzania, Uganda, among others. Improve technology deployment has also played a large role in enabling these discoveries, with some of Africa's developments in the deep offshore rivaling that of those in the Gulf of Mexico.

While natural gas was not too long ago considered a nuisance byproduct in sub-Saharan Africa, the resource is increasingly utilized in large scale operations such as LNG, power generation and trans-border pipelines, and also in smaller scale applications such as LPG and CNG. With the known natural gas reserves across North Africa and new discoveries in sub-Sahara, the continent is a natural gas player to be reckoned with. In Mozambique and Tanzania alone, there is reasonable confidence that the two areas together hold a resource of at least 190 Tcf with expectations that proven reserves could more than double with further exploration.

And the shale boom is not exclusive to North America, Africa too has her share of unconventional resources. Shale oil, shale gas, and coal bed methane are all now receiving attention from both governments and the private sector and a number of projects are afoot.

As for alternative energy, there are literally hundreds of small-scale projects established and in the works, not to mention the dozens of larger scale projects on the drawing board; these translate into billions of dollars in investment. The sector is making progress with new, renewable-specific legislation emerging in many countries, facilitating development of the industry.

In addition to the major wind farm and solar projects online or under construction in Egypt, Ethiopia, Kenya, Morocco, and South Africa, the continent's hydropower resource is enormous with some estimates having it accounting for 12% of the world's potential. Ethiopia is looking to develop 6 GW of power with its Grand Renaissance Dam, the Chinese are already heavily invested in Africa's hydropower and are funding $500 million toward Cote d'Ivoire's 275-MW Soubre Dam, and the Grand Inga scheme in the Democratic Republic of Congo will be the world's largest if plans are implemented as envisioned. Not to be left behind is geothermal. Kenya is set to construct new geothermal power plants by December 2015, and in fact, its strategy would make it the world's number one geothermal producer by 2033 if executed accordingly.

Having a near-term, tangible impact in improving the lives of Africans are the many small scale, off-grid rural projects. These projects are varied and include household solar products, community waste to energy, roof top solar and wind, and biofuel and biogas applications. Perhaps the greatest achievement over the decade has been seen in the manufacturing sector with solar factories emerging to meet growing regional solar demand. This trend has led to a technology transfer with Africans learning to provide services to their communities. Many of the projects have allowed typical low-income villagers to become small business owners and in turn pass on that technology to their communities. This development is certainly a success story for the continent by any measure.

In closing, the hydrocarbon and renewable initiatives set forth by African governments as well as by their partners from around the globe, are paying huge dividends. While much progress has been made, there is a long road ahead to bring Africans up to a first world standard of living, and American know-how and investment can play a major role in making that happen.

---

71

Mr. SMITH. Ms. Sutherland, thank you very much for your testimony and for your insights and your expertise.

I would like to now yield to Ms. Bass.

Ms. BASS. And thank you. I appreciate you going out of sequence for a minute. I really just wanted to ask a couple of questions.

But I first want to address my colleague, Representative Stockman, you know, your concerns that you were raising about China.

And I think one of the first things that we can do, hopefully before lame duck is over, is take care of two things, the Power Africa that is over in the Senate and then also AGOA.

You know, I mean, because to the extent that we can increase our participation—because I know I have heard from many, many African countries how much they do want to do business with us, but, you know, sometimes we put our own roadblocks up.

Mr. STOCKMAN. Exactly.

Ms. BASS. Exactly.

So, Mr. Williams, I just wanted to ask—I was asking the first panel about Power Africa and its reach into urban areas, in the residential areas, not the commercial, and, also, in the rural areas.

And you, you know, representing civil society, I just wanted to know your take on the same question I had asked the first panel.

Mr. WILLIAMS. Well, I believe—and it is anecdotal, to some extent—but I do believe, having come out of the U.S.-Africa ministerial and looking at the effective role and the amount of discussion that we talked about with grids, mini grids, and getting electricity into rural areas.

And then, at the leaders' summit, I attended a session that GE put on called Africa Rising, and there were many, many entrepreneurial-type things. By "entrepreneurial," I mean they are sustainable.

In other words, they were going into rural communities and creating opportunities for young people to supply electricity and make a little bit of money to keep it going and keep their incentives up.

So it is happening and it—and it could be expedited, but it is happening and it is part of—when you get to Beyond the Grid, part of the Power Africa agenda to expand this.

Ms. BASS. Thank you.

And maybe, Ms. Sutherland, you would like to respond to that as well.

Ms. SUTHERLAND. I am sorry. I thought the question was addressed to my colleague. Can you repeat that again, please.

Ms. BASS. Oh, yeah. It was, but it was to you, too.

I was just wondering your opinions on how Power Africa and our efforts of reaching beyond commercial areas and going into urban residential and rural areas.

Ms. SUTHERLAND. I am not that familiarized with that aspect of the industry, as my focus is on the petroleum industry.

However, I do know that the African communities do appreciate American investment. There is absolutely other investment available to them from the likes of China, but they do like dealing with the Americans better.

And I know that there are several small-scale projects emanating from the United States supplying off-grid solutions such as, you know, the solar lanterns, replacing the kerosene, the clean cooking stoves, and they are really quite receptive.

Ms. BASS. Thank you.

Mr. SMITH. I will go out of order and I will recognize Mr. Stockman. Then I will go third.

Mr. STOCKMAN. Yeah. I am glad you are from Houston. I represent Houston, and, as you know, fracking was a critical part of George Mitchell's portfolio, and I think that he really changed and revolutionized the world when he developed the advanced fracking.

And I think we lost her. That's okay.

I would like to ask, Mr. Williams, on our side, you are free market. Can you be blunt enough to tell me how is it that we are impeding, in what ways we can undo something to make it more beneficial for both sides.

I mean, how is the Government—you know, a lot of times we have passed laws here that had very well-intended meaning, but, ultimately, it ends up impacting your industry or other industries, quite frankly, in a negative way. And I would like to know what laws we passed that were meant to be for good that are not.

Mr. WILLIAMS. Well, in response and to be undiplomatic, I mean, I don't think anyone ever passes a law that they don't think it is not going to work the way they intend it to work. So we will start with that premise.

The thing that I feel that we miss out on is that we don't really listen to the beneficiaries. I am talking about in the U.S. The U.S. has great reach. If I was to ask an African energy minister, to pick up your conversation about China, who they would like to work with, unanimously it would be with the United States.

But we do put in place not the law, but then it is the policy, how the law is going to be implemented, that creates obstacles. And the obstacles, in a global economy—now, remember, oil is a global economy, supply and demand. And so no one country really can control that whole industry.

But if—so if we put up—if we put obstacles up, it goes to where there are less obstacles or they can get what they consider to be a fairer shot, but the preference—for instance, if an energy minister comes here and they want to work on something and they would prefer to work with the U.S. Department of Energy, oftentimes they have to go the State Department. And then that means they have to involve their Minister of Foreign Affairs, and they would prefer to keep it in the house—the energy house.

So some of the things that we do create obstacles for us going forward. And then there are issues within some of our agencies where we can't be as supportive as the private sector would like because of regulations that are in place and the agencies themselves don't want to necessarily show favoritism to Company A over Company B. And so, in some respects, the playing field is not level and our industries don't get the benefit of what we could do.

Mr. STOCKMAN. Yeah, we can just look at—and no offense to the State Department, the previous panel, but you can look at the time and length it has taken just to discuss a pipeline here in the United States.

Mr. WILLIAMS. Yeah.

Mr. STOCKMAN. And it is unfortunate that the State Department is interceding in free commerce, but I see it repeatedly. As you know, this is years ago, I met with the DRC's energy minister, and that was a complaint back 15, 18 years ago, and it hasn't been resolved. And I am not going to be here in January. I want to work as an intern for Congressman Smith, but my hope is that we can do some kind of legislation to where we step back and allow companies to work together.

And it is absolutely true, by the way, they do want to work with American companies. They feel like we get a fair shake from Americans. They also, Americans do something that the Chinese don't; the Americans will employee local labor and train them in the technologies and the skills, and they even invest in infrastructure. They love that. But the Chinese are more parochial. They will bring in their own labor, as you know, and their own labor is almost, in itself, they are locked up, and they don't even get to intermingle.

So I would request, if you have time or you can administratively get us back some of the policies you think—and you don't have to be diplomatic. It is just you, me, and Connie Chung, we will keep it secret. If you can get us some of the things that Congressman Smith down the road could facilitate where we are doing a better job of trying to help our industries, I would appreciate that. I think some frankness would be in order here.

Mr. WILLIAMS. Well, you know, take Power Africa, again. I mean, you just don't say I want to turn on that switch. I mean, it takes years to develop some of these infrastructure projects. But the country needs the electricity now.

Mr. STOCKMAN. Yes.

Mr. WILLIAMS. And we have a lot of technology we can come in and drop, almost instant generators and tie it right into the grid and start to feed it while we are building out the more permanent, sustainable power supply. So I mean, there are a lot of things, and I am happy to respond to you with some of those kind of shortcut thoughts that I have about how we can be more effective.

Mr. STOCKMAN. I am so on your side. I go nuts when I go visit there because I really want to help them. I have great compassion for them and they want what the rest of the world wants, and yet I see time and time our Government is interceding in a way that is disruptive and harmful for the very people we claim to want to help. And I just am thrilled that you have dedicated your life to this, and I really appreciate the sacrifices you have made. And I apologize for the bureaucracy and the inconsistency from our side.

Mr. WILLIAMS. Well, I appreciate that, but I also want to say, I got a lot of help from the U.S. side. Don't get me wrong.

Mr. STOCKMAN. Well, I know that, but——

Mr. WILLIAMS. And I have come and I have knocked on the door and I have received some help.

Mr. STOCKMAN. But we can do better.

Mr. WILLIAMS. Okay.

Mr. STOCKMAN. When I go there and I hear privately some of the conversations I hear from their side, their government officials, it is—excuse my expression—but I am really—I used profanity there, consider it used—I am really upset that we are, time and time again, shooting ourselves in the foot.

With that, I yield back to the chairman.

Mr. SMITH. Mr. Stockman, thank you very much.

Just a few final questions and, Mr. Williams, thank you very much for your testimony and again for your leadership.

Can you tell us, do you have any insight as to how the participants, especially nongovernment actors were selected for the ministerial? You made a very good point about the importance of Power Africa, having Diaspora and women-owned businesses involved. And I am wondering, who does the selection? Is it self-selection, people know that it is coming and they get themselves onto a list and then have access, or is it by invitation only?

Secondly, the issue—and I will ask this of Ms. Sutherland when she gets back on, but you might want to speak to it as well—for most of my career in Congress, I have been in Congress for 34 years now. I have been an ardent proponent of waste-to-energy initiatives, believing that it obviously takes care of municipal garbage while it also produces clean energy, and with modern technology being what it is, what it comes out of, that smokestack at the end of the day is as pristine as it possibly can be. It is not always perfect, obviously, but with the right controls and the right environmental safeguards, it is cleaner.

And we know that, you know, as a continent and the countries matriculate to being an industrialized continent or nation, people want to cut corners. There is going to be much waste. Industrial waste is one thing but municipal waste will grow in number. And what do you do with it?

And I am wondering how well you think Power Africa is incorporating the waste-to-energy initiatives as a way of powering up Africa as part of a mix.

And let me also ask you, you know, I did ask the earlier panel, and I think they will get back with some insights, but I am very worried about cybersecurity issues and about terrorism. It doesn't take much if improper safeguards are not followed, whereby a whole infrastructure can be demolished very, very quickly.

And Ms. Sutherland, I guess she's still not on, but she had spoken about China, and we all know that China demands a great deal of repayment, usually. I mean, in Ghana they get the oil and have access to that oil. We know that countries like Sudan and others, very often weapons are in the mix in exchange for their raw materials, especially oil there.

And I am wondering, you know, if you feel we have competed well enough with the People's Republic of China to say, as both my good friend, Mr. Stockman, and others have said, the Africans and you as well want to deal with the United States of America and with our private sector as well. But if we are not in the game, who do they turn to? They turn to the Chinese. Have we turned to corner, or are the Chinese still outcompeting us on the continent?

Mr. WILLIAMS. Thank you, Mr. Chairman. For your first question on the U.S.-Africa Energy Ministerial, Leadership Africa was responsible for the outreach in the marketing of that event that took place in Ethiopia. The U.S. Department of Energy handled the government agency participation, those agencies who did come to Ethiopia to participate.

Now, I can tell you, intentionally, we reached out to everybody. We went to Commerce Department. We got lists from all of the agencies, and small businesses, large businesses, so we made it inclusive, and then we made it easy for even the African businessmen to attend, and we had different price referential so that they had to pay something, but it was a pittance, so that we made sure that it was a meeting that had both African and U.S. businesses participating and benefiting. So it was on us, if there is complaints about who could not come, who couldn't get there, it is on Leadership Africa USA.

Your second question was waste-to-energy. We have seen, over the years, because we are an NGO, a number of waste-to-energy projects that work in rural communities, where there is the collection now of waste and it is the co-generation of waste to turning it into energy. They are very effective, particularly with plastic. You will find it in Egypt. There is a huge project going on.

In fact, we were working with another NGO and they had a competition on an annualized basis. And a lot of the people who won those competitions were dealing with energy but they were dealing with removing waste, and it was at the university level. So, I mean, it is attractive to young people but it is attractive for young people in rural communities, if they can clean up their communities and also have some money coming from that and it generates electricity. It is a win-win for everybody.

Mr. SMITH. Just a couple of final questions, and then, Mr. Stockman, do you have anything to conclude?

Dr. Ichord, in response to my question about gaps, listed five. One of them was the urban subnational part and I asked whether or not we are reaching out to state and local governments, and he said that is becoming more and more important. And I wonder if you might want to speak to that, obviously we should work with the central government but we shouldn't be capital-centric. Look to those other key players. You might want to expand upon that.

And the competition with China, if you could touch on that one.

And finally, how do we measure success? You know, will we know it when we see it, or are there metrics that can be employed to say, okay, we have now seen such and such number of municipalities and people gain access to electricity? Does anybody have a backdrop in mind to determine whether or not we are succeeding in this effort?

Mr. WILLIAMS. Okay. Picking up on the China question.

Mr. SMITH. Yes.

Mr. WILLIAMS. It is the glass is half-full/half-empty kind of a thing. China has a totally different system than we have. They go at it differently. I mean, when you are talking to a company that says we are a Chinese company, you don't know if it is a Chinese company or if the company is partially owned by the government or representing the government. So when you put our companies into that mix, it is hard to compete.

And then there was reference earlier to the Foreign Corrupt Practices Act and clarification and clarity on what, when you are working within the bounds, everyone wants to work within the bounds so that you are very clear that the activities that you are undertaking are not going to put you afoul of that law would be very helpful. We can overcome what I think is China's vast amount of financing that they have available because we really make better partners. We are there for the long run. And I think that the African governments understand that.

And we need to work—to pick up on your second question—we need to move it out of the leadership in the heads of the ministries and the government officials and move it into a level where we are talking to the business people who, like business people here, can go talk to the government but they need the support and the help and assistance that we could provide them.

Mr. SMITH. I see Ms. Sutherland is back so I just would ask her: You mentioned the Cote d'Ivoire issue in China. So a more general question would be, how well or poorly are we competing, in your opinion, with Chinese initiatives?

And you had also mentioned the waste-to-energy, which is something that I just asked Mr. Williams before you came back on. How widespread are those projects, which obviously do two great things at one time, produce energy but also take care of a municipal waste problem? Landfills, as we all know, are ticking time bombs because of what they do to aquifers and to water systems as they leach.

So if you could respond to those two, I would appreciate it.

Ms. SUTHERLAND. Okay. As far as how are we competing with China, we are competing pretty well with China; however, as others have mentioned, the transparency issue is very big in Africa, but there are only, I believe, 17 or 18 countries who have signed up to the EITI. So for those who have not yet signed up to it or who have not met the requirements to be approved, Chinese money is very attractive and it comes with very little strings attached to it. And that is just a fact. It is very attractive to some African governments.

On the other hand, Chinese technology, while it has vastly improved over the last decade, is still lagging behind American technology. And many of the savvier national oil companies in Africa would much rather prefer to work with American services firms and oil and gas exploration companies.

As regards to waste-to-energy, projects are popping up all over the continent. They are small-scale and medium-scale. I know of one project, it is waste-to-energy that comes from a prison facility and that waste-to-energy powers that facility. There is also animal-waste-to-energy as well as municipal-waste-to-energy. So municipal-waste-to-energy has very high potential in the continent, and I believe you will see many more projects cropping up as investment comes along and the technology transfer is made to these countries.

Mr. SMITH. Thank you so very much for coming back online and——

Ms. SUTHERLAND. Sorry about that. Technology fails us sometimes.

Mr. SMITH. Let me just ask you, hydropower is still a major factor in African energy planning but major projects such as Ethiopia's Grand Renaissance Dam have regional implications that make it politically difficult. How do countries such as Ethiopia and

Egypt deal with conflicts over such major power and water projects? First, give me your background in Egypt.

Ms. SUTHERLAND. It is basically a governmental power play. I don't think that the Ethiopia project would have made it as far as it has if it weren't for the Arab Spring and, you know, the resulting multiple governments and disarray in Egypt. Generally, I think that you would have seen that project not advance as far as it has. Had Egypt not had its difficulties, it would probably still be a debate amongst the countries, I would say, for several years to come. And that being said, you may find Egypt in the not-too-distant future trying to go in and circumvent the progress that has been made.

Mr. SMITH. And one final question to both of you: 10 years from now, can you make any kind of guesstimate or projection as to how many people on the continent will have access to electricity?

Ms. SUTHERLAND. In the next decade?

Mr. SMITH. Yes.

Ms. SUTHERLAND. I don't see a huge increase. I would say maybe a 15 percent increase in the next decade if the major alternative energy projects come to fruition, such as the geothermal and the hydropower.

Mr. SMITH. Okay. Mr. Williams?

Mr. WILLIAMS. Well, the statistics that I—I have to share her assessment——

Mr. SMITH. Right.

Mr. WILLIAMS [continuing]. That there is not going to be a substantial number of people who will have access to electricity in Africa if we stay on the current level that we are on right now. It is estimated by 2040 you still may have 500 million people on the continent without electricity.

Mr. SMITH. And it is 590 million right now, right?

Mr. WILLIAMS. Yeah.

Mr. SMITH. Approximately. Thank you. That means we need to accelerate and beef up our efforts, and I think we end on that point.

Anything you would like to add, Mr. Williams, before we end?

Mr. WILLIAMS. No, I just want to thank you for the opportunity and the privilege to be here and to testify. I am hopeful that some of the things that I said and I will be back to you and hope to—and applaud your leadership, both you and Congressman Stockman. Thank you so much.

Mr. SMITH. Thank you.

Mr. STOCKMAN. Thank you very much.

Mr. SMITH. The hearing is adjourned, and thank you very much.

Mr. WILLIAMS. Thank you.

[Whereupon, at 3:14 p.m., the subcommittee was adjourned.]

# APPENDIX

---

## SUBCOMMITTEE HEARING NOTICE
## COMMITTEE ON FOREIGN AFFAIRS
U.S. HOUSE OF REPRESENTATIVES
WASHINGTON, DC 20515-6128

**Subcommittee on Africa, Global Health, Global Human Rights, and International Organizations**
**Christopher H. Smith (R-NJ), Chairman**

November 14, 2014

**TO:  MEMBERS OF THE COMMITTEE ON FOREIGN AFFAIRS**

You are respectfully requested to attend an OPEN hearing of the Committee on Foreign Affairs, to be held by the Subcommittee on Africa, Global Health, Global Human Rights, and International Organizations in Room 2172 of the Rayburn House Office Building (and available live on the Committee website at www.foreignaffairs.house.gov):

**DATE:**              Friday, November 14, 2014

**TIME:**              12:00 p.m.

**SUBJECT:**           The Future of Energy in Africa

**WITNESSES:**         Panel I
                       Robert F. Ichord, Jr., Ph.D.
                       Deputy Assistant Secretary
                       Bureau of Energy Resources
                       U.S. Department of State

                       The Honorable Eric G. Postel
                       Assistant to the Administrator
                       Bureau for Africa
                       U.S. Agency for International Development

                       Mr. Jonathan Elkind
                       Acting Assistant Secretary
                       Office of International Affairs
                       U.S. Department of Energy

                       Panel II
                       Mr. Walker A. Williams
                       President and Chief Executive Officer
                       Leadership Africa USA

                       Ms. Dianne R. Sutherland
                       Owner and Publisher
                       Petroleum Africa Magazine
                       *(Appearing via videoconference)*

### By Direction of the Chairman

*The Committee on Foreign Affairs seeks to make its facilities accessible to persons with disabilities. If you are in need of special accommodations, please call 202/225-5021 at least four business days in advance of the event, whenever practicable. Questions with regard to special accommodations in general (including availability of Committee materials in alternative formats and assistive listening devices) may be directed to the Committee.*

# COMMITTEE ON FOREIGN AFFAIRS

MINUTES OF SUBCOMMITTEE ON _Africa, Global Health, Global Human Rights, and International Organizations_ HEARING

Day___ _Friday_ ___Date__ _November 14, 2014_ ___Room _2172 Rayburn HOB_

Starting Time ___ _12:57 p.m._ ___Ending Time ___ _3:14 p.m._

Recesses | _0_ | (___to___)(___to___)(___to___)(___to___)(___to___)(___to___)

---

**Presiding Member(s)**

_Rep. Chris Smith, Rep. Randy Weber_

---

_Check all of the following that apply:_

Open Session ☑
Executive (closed) Session ☐
Televised ☑

Electronically Recorded (taped) ☑
Stenographic Record ☑

---

**TITLE OF HEARING:**

_The Future of Energy in Africa_

---

**SUBCOMMITTEE MEMBERS PRESENT:**

_Rep. Steve Stockman, Rep. David Cicilline, Rep. Karen Bass_

---

**NON-SUBCOMMITTEE MEMBERS PRESENT:** _(Mark with an * if they are not members of full committee.)_

---

**HEARING WITNESSES: Same as meeting notice attached? Yes ☑ No ☐**
_(If "no", please list below and include title, agency, department, or organization.)_

---

**STATEMENTS FOR THE RECORD:** _(List any statements submitted for the record.)_

_Responses to Rep. Chris Smith's questions for the record from Eric Postel of USAID_
_Response to Rep. Karen Bass' request for information from the Department of Energy_
_Statement for the record from Ms. Dana Hyde of the Millennium Challenge Corporation, submitted by Rep. Chris Smith_

---

TIME SCHEDULED TO RECONVENE _____
or
TIME ADJOURNED ___ _3:14 p.m._

_Gregory B. Simpkins_
**Subcommittee Staff Director**

FROM THE AMERICAN PEOPLE

December 2, 2014

Dear Congressman Smith,

Thank you for chairing the recent hearing on the Future of Energy in Africa on November 14th in the Subcommittee on Africa, Global Health, Global Human Rights and International Organizations. Your dedicated leadership on issues to improve the lives of people in Africa, including efforts to increase production of and provide more effective access to energy in Africa, is deeply appreciated.

As you rightly noted during the hearing, electrification in Africa faces great operational, regulatory, and investment challenges. The Power Africa initiative strives to address these barriers. As you know, Power Africa exemplifies a new model of development where our nation's convening power is used to leverage innovative partnerships with African governments, the private sector, and other partners to make quick-impact interventions and investments in electricity generation throughout in Sub-Saharan Africa. The Electrify Africa Act of 2014 you cosponsored and championed in Congress supports these efforts.

Thank you specifically for asking about the expertise of African energy and power sector leaders. As I mentioned during the hearing, USAID maintains agreements with the U.S. Energy Association (USEA) and the National Association of Regulatory Utility Commissioners (NARUC). These entities have both regional and bilateral country programs in Sub-Saharan Africa that work to narrow technical shortfalls and improve capabilities. You will find more detailed examples of how these programs operate attached.

Rest assured that while I am at USAID I will continue to work on the ongoing challenges of energy access in Sub-Saharan Africa. My staff and I are ready and available to address any questions or concerns you may have in the future. Thank you again for your continued leadership on energy issues in Africa and development issues on the continent broadly.

Sincerely,

Eric G. Postel
Assistant to the Administrator for Africa

U.S. Agency for International Development
1300 Pennsylvania Avenue, NW
Washington, DC 20523
www.usaid.gov

**ATTACHMENT**

**USAID Assistant to the Administrator Eric Postel's Responses to
Congressman Chris Smith's Questions
at the Hearing on the Future of Energy in Africa on November 14, 2014**

**Question: Please provide background on USEA and NARUC partnerships. Who has participated under Power Africa? Does training on critical infrastructure protection take place under these partnerships?**

**Answer:** USAID has cooperative agreements with the U.S. Energy Association (USEA) and the National Association of Regulatory Utility Commissioners (NARUC) which have both regional and bilateral country programs in sub-Saharan Africa. USAID supports USEA's Energy Utility Partnership Program, its Transmission System Planning Partnership and East Africa Geothermal Partnership and NARUC's Energy Regulatory Partnership Program. As part of MCC's $498.2 million power compact with Ghana to fight poverty by transforming the country's energy sector, MCC provided funding in the past and plans to fund a NARUC bilateral program in Ghana. Currently, NARUC has regional programs in place in West, East, and Southern Africa and bilateral programs underway in Tanzania and Ethiopia. USEA has regional programs in East Africa and bilateral programs in Ghana, Ethiopia, Kenya and Tanzania.

As examples of how these programs operate, in Tanzania, USEA has brought in U.S. utility experts from Bonneville Power Administration (BPA), Pacificorp, Portland General Electric, Sacramento Municipal Utility District, and New England Electric System (National Grid) to undertake a series of assessments, workshops, and exchanges on transmission system operational issues and procedures. In the case of NARUC, there is a regulatory partnership in place between the Illinois Commerce Commission and the Energy and Water Utilities Regulatory Authority (EWURA) in Tanzania. In December 2014, NARUC will launch a partnership between the Missouri Public Service Commission and the Ethiopia Energy Authority (EEA). NARUC also has an Energy Regulatory Partnership with the Nigerian Electricity Regulatory Commission (NERC).

In Nigeria, prospective investors and purchasers of the successor generation companies were mandated through the request for proposal documents to submit bids for the power plants through a consortium that would comprise technical partners. The investors, or project sponsors in the case of green field power generation plants, do not necessarily need technical knowledge of the sector to operate a power plant. Investors typically procure the technical service to operate a power plant through an operations and maintenance (O&M) contract.

To provide training to the existing staff of the successor companies on key issues in O&M, USAID together with USEA organized a workshop in Lagos, Nigeria, on Reducing Power Outages and Improving Electric Services in October 2013 for senior and middle level staff, as well as the new owners. The workshop was designed to build capacity to implement loss reduction programs in the successor companies. All the privatized distribution companies were invited for the training workshop and a large percentage. As a follow up to the training, U.S. Trade and Development Agency (USTDA) selected approximately four of the distribution companies for a reverse trade mission in the U.S. Two American companies participated in the training including ABB Ventyx, which has its headquarters in Houston, TX, and Goodworks International, with offices in Washington, D.C., and Atlanta, GA.

At the regional level in East Africa, NARUC launched in October 2014 the East Africa Regional Regulatory Partnership to enhance the legal, technical and regulatory frameworks for regional power trade in the Eastern Africa Power Pool (EAPP) countries and ultimately strengthen regulatory frameworks that promote an enabling environment for investment and infrastructure as well as energy transactions. USEA also launched in August the East Africa Transmission Planning Partnership (EATP) with the EAPP to improve the capacity of transmission planners in Kenya, Ethiopia and Tanzania to develop regional electric power transmission corridors that will serve as the backbone infrastructure for the cross-border trade and exchange of electricity, the majority of which will come from renewable sources.

With USAID funding, the USEA East Africa Geothermal Partnership and African Union Commission recently hosted 35 government and private sector representatives from six East African nations - Djibouti, Ethiopia, Kenya, Rwanda, Tanzania and Uganda · · on a six day geothermal road show in the U.S. that included attendance at the 38th Geothermal Resources Council (GRC) annual meeting in Portland, Oregon, meetings with private geothermal companies in Reno, Nevada and with U.S. government officials and public and private project developers in Washington, DC.

**See also Tab 1 and Tab 2 for a List of Regulators in Africa that NARUC is assisting and a List of Companies Involved in Power Africa Exchanges with USEA.**

**Question: How do we take into account security concerns (terrorism, etc) in our planning?**

**Answer:** Regarding the physical security of critical infrastructure, Power Africa is driven by private sector investment for project development and implementation in the electrical generation, transmission, and distribution sectors. Power Africa looks to strengthen the enabling policy and market conditions for these investments to thrive in partnership with host country governments and other stakeholders, while private sector owners of power sector assets devote significant efforts to ensure that operational considerations including physical security, are addressed in their planning efforts. Additionally, Power Africa and earlier efforts to strengthen the power sector in Africa have increased the capacity of utilities and regulators to oversee and operate power grids in their respective countries through direct engagement and partnerships with NARUC and USEA. These efforts will help these entities more effectively manage major grid collapses and faults and increase overall stability of the grid.

**Tab 1 - List of Regulators in Africa that NARUC is assisting**

- Energy and Water Utilities Regulatory Authority (EWURA) - Tanzania
- Independent Regulatory Board (IRB) of the Eastern Africa Power Pool (EAPP)
- Ethiopia Energy Authority (EEA)
- Energy Regulatory Commission (ERC) – Kenya
- Nigerian Electricity Regulatory Commission (NERC)

**Tab 2 - List of Companies Involved in Power Africa Exchanges with USEA**

| | Company/Organization |
|---|---|
| FY13 | SAPP Exchange on Ancillary Services Market |
| | Federal Energy Regulatory Commission |
| | PJM Interconnection |
| | New York Independent System Operator |
| | North American Electric Reliability Council |
| | Georgia Power |
| | Alabama Power |
| | Siemens |
| | Botswana Power Corp |
| | Societe Nationale d'Electricite |
| | Lesotho Electricity Company |
| | Electricity Supply Corporation of Malawi |
| | Electricidade do Mozambique |
| | Hidroelectrica de Cahora Bassa |
| | Mozambique Transmission Company |
| | Namibia Power Corporation |
| | Eskom |
| | Swaziland Electricity Company |
| | Tanzania Electric Supply Company Limited (TANESCO) |
| | Zimbabwe Electricity Transmission and Distribution Company |
| | Southern African Power Pool Coordination Centre |
| FY13 | US-East Africa Geothermal Partnership |
| | Dewhurst Group |
| | Geothermal Resources Group |
| | GeothermEx |
| | Power Engineers |
| | Geothermal Development Associates |
| | Atlas Geosciences, Inc. |
| | EGS, Inc. |
| | TAS Energy, Inc. |
| | Lawrence Berkeley National Lab |
| | Thermochem, Inc |

| | | |
|---|---|---|
| | | GeoGlobal Energy |
| | | Cumming Geoscience |
| | | Geologica, Inc |
| | | Panorama Environmental |
| | | Allman Group |
| | | Global Power Solutions |
| | | Dormin, Inc. |
| | | Barker Engineering |
| | | ZESCO |
| | | National Electricity Company (Comoros) |
| | | Geothermal Development Company (GDC) |
| | | VASTU co. Ltd. |
| | | KenGen |
| | | IPSK |
| | | Sosian Energy Ltd |
| FY13 | | Tanzania Partnership |
| | | TANESCO |
| | | ZECO |
| | | Hunton and Williams, LLP |
| | | Kentucky Public Service Commission |
| | | National Grid |
| | | Sacramento Municipal Utility District |
| FY14 | | NIGERIA WORKSHOP NAPTIN |
| | | MERALCO |
| | | CESC |
| | | TP DDL |
| | | GE |
| | | Itron |
| | | SEL |
| | | Tetra Tech |
| | | ABB |
| | | UEDCL |
| | | Mein River Power Company |
| | | Liberia Electricity Corporation |
| | | Electricity Company of Ghana |

88

| | | |
|---|---|---|
| | | TANESCO |
| | | Kenya Power |
| | | Ethiopian Electric Power Corporation |
| | | NERC |
| | | NBET |
| | | IBADAN EDC |
| | | KADUNA EDC |
| | | BENIN EDC |
| | | KANO EDC |
| | | EKO EDC |
| | | PH EDC |
| | | JOS EDC |
| | | IKEJA EDC |
| | | YOLA EDC |
| | | ABUJA EDC |
| | | ENUGU EDC |
| | | NAPTIN CHQ |
| FY14 | | US-East Africa Geothermal Partnership |
| | | Ram Energy |
| | | Athena Global Alliance (Amanda Lonsdale) |
| | | Locke Lord, LLP |
| | | Geothermal Development Company (GDC) |
| | | KenGen |
| | | Ethiopian Electric Power (EEP) |
| | | Symbion Power Tanzania |
| | | Symbion Power, LLC. |
| | | Reykjavik Geothermal |
| | | Geothermal Resource Group (GRG) |
| | | Geothermal Resources Council (GRC) |
| | | Toshiba |
| | | ElectraTherm |
| | | Dewhurst Group |
| | | GreenFire Energy |
| | | Industrial Cooling Systems |
| | | POWER Engineers |

| | |
|---|---|
| | GreenMax Capital Advisors |
| | ORMAT |
| | Geologica Inc. |
| | Veizades Group |
| | Leidos |
| | ENEL Green Power North America (Subsidiary of ENEL) |
| | TransCentury Limited |
| | Soslan Energy |
| | Allman Group/Langson Energy |
| | Baker Hughes |
| | Accurate Power Systems Ltd. (Kenyan) |
| | Energy Development Corporation Ltd. (Rwanda, formerly part of EWSA) |
| | InfraTech (Tanzania) |
| | COPI Development (Cameroon) |
| | ODDEG (Office of geothermal energy development for Djibouti) |
| | EGS Inc. |
| | Industrial Builders |
| | Capuano Engineering |
| | Turboden/Mitsubishi |
| | EleQtra |
| | Investec Holdings |
| | Aldwych Capital |
| | Aquarius Global Energy Partners / Cornerstone Energy Solutions |
| FY14 | Tanzania Partnership |
| | Tata Power Delhi Distribution Limited (TPDDL) |
| | Power Grid Corporation of India Limited (PGCIL) |
| | Portland General Electric |
| | Sacramento Municipal Utility District (SMUD) |
| | New England Electric System (National Grid) |
| | TR Energy Services |
| | Rosewood Energy Consulting |
| | Northern Indiana Public Service Company |
| | Cadmus Group |
| | ICF International |
| | Southern California Gas Company |

| | | |
|---|---|---|
| | | Tata Power |
| | | Power Grid Corporation of India Limited (POWERGRID) |
| | | Power System Operation Corporation Limited (POSOCO) |
| FY14 | | Metering, Billing & Loss Reduction: A Regional Workshop for Distribution Utilities |
| | | GE Energy Management |
| | | Alstom |
| | | Industrial Promotion Services (IPS) - Uganda |
| | | Visayan Electric Company (VECO) |
| | | Itron |
| | | Calcutta Electric Supply Company |
| | | Kenya Power and Light Company |
| | | Eskom |
| | | Manila Electricity Company (MERALCO) |
| | | Ibadan Electricity Distribution Company (IBEDC) |
| | | West Nile Rural Electrification Company (WENRECO) |
| | | Swaziland Electricity Company (SEC) |
| | | Electricity Company of Ghana |
| FY14 | | Kenya Wind Integration |
| | | Nexant |
| | | Sacramento Municipal Utility District (SMUD) |
| | | KenGen |
| | | Kenya Power and Light Company |
| | | Kenya Electricity Transmission Company |
| | | Xcel Energy |
| | | Northern States Power Company |
| | | Public Service Company of Colorado |
| | | Southwestern Public Service |
| | | California Independent System Operation (CAISO) |
| | | Western Area Power Authority |
| | | Rocky Mountain Reserve Group |
| | | Incsys |
| | | Puget Sound Energy |
| | | Bonneville Power Administration |
| | | Northwest Power Pool |
| | | Utility System Efficiencies |

Further information from the Department of Energy requested by Rep. Karen Bass on Making Global Local

In response to dramatic shifts in the global economy, U.S. companies are increasingly targeting emerging markets as export destinations. Given its unique role, the U.S. Trade and Development Agency is supporting U.S. businesses interested in entering or expanding their presence in developing and middle-income countries through its Making Global Local initiative.

The foundation of Making Global Local is formed by strategic partnerships between the Agency and local business and economic development organizations located throughout the United States. By understanding USTDA's programs and priorities, these partner organizations are helping companies in their communities identify sales opportunities abroad through various USTDA-funded activities.

By working together, USTDA and its partner organizations are supporting the creation of high-paying local jobs through the growth of U.S. exports. Since Making Global Local was launched on World Trade Day in 2012, USTDA and its partner organizations have co-hosted conferences, industry roundtables, webinars, and provided joint marketing for each other's events.

MATERIAL SUBMITTED FOR THE RECORD BY THE HONORABLE CHRISTOPHER H. SMITH, A REPRESENTATIVE IN CONGRESS FROM THE STATE OF NEW JERSEY, AND CHAIRMAN, SUBCOMMITTEE ON AFRICA, GLOBAL HEALTH, GLOBAL HUMAN RIGHTS, AND INTERNATIONAL ORGANIZATIONS

*The Future of Energy in Africa*
**House Foreign Affairs Subcommittee on Africa, Global Health, Global Human Rights, and International Organizations**
**November 14, 2014**

**Statement for the Record**
**Dana J. Hyde**
**Chief Executive Officer, Millennium Challenge Corporation**

Chairman Smith, Ranking Member Bass and Members of the Africa Subcommittee:

On behalf of the Millennium Challenge Corporation (MCC), I appreciate this opportunity to describe our important contributions to the future of Africa's energy sector as we work to build the physical infrastructure and improve the policy environments needed to create sustainable economic growth.

MCC's mission, as you know, is to reduce poverty in those countries that are relatively well governed though our competitive selection process, country-owned implementation approach and focus on results. Since its establishment by Congress 10 years ago, MCC has funded programs across a wide variety of sectors and disciplines of international development. The common thread across MCC's commitments – whether a port in Benin, land tenure programs in Burkina Faso, education in Namibia, or a submarine power cable between Zanzibar and mainland Tanzania – is that economic analysis and country commitment underpin sector and project choices.

## Why and How MCC invests in energy in Africa

For many of our Africa partners, one of their major constraints to economic growth is their lack of reliable power, and they are committing to tackling this constraint. This means investing in energy infrastructure, implementing tough policy and regulatory reforms, and engaging in institutional capacity-building in the power sector. As a condition for our investments, MCC is prepared to insist our partners take on the tough reforms critical to increase private sector investment opportunities and diminish opportunities for corruption. This approach works because MCC's country selection process is designed to identify only those low income countries most committed to a sound policy environment. We also look for ways to facilitate clean, off-grid energy generation and improve the investment climate for renewable energy.

Working hand-in-hand with partner countries and the private sector, in addition to funding large infrastructure grants, MCC is:
- helping clear the way for businesses to invest in power projects that will grow economies and fight poverty across the continent;
- assisting governments prepare potential projects, while also helping establish regulatory and institutional structures that are needed to attract and protect private investments; and
- helping American companies invest in some of the fastest-growing economies in the world by pursuing fair, open and transparent procurements.

MCC has been funding energy projects in Africa since 2008, when MCC funded approximately $200 million in Tanzanian power sector investments. As a requirement of this compact, the Government of Tanzania passed the first comprehensive revision to an electricity law dating back to 1931, a law which had been far too dated to address current market needs. As a result of MCC's engagement with the government through the compact, Tanzanian regulators approved new, more cost-reflective tariffs, a key step for attracting private investment in the power sector. MCC is currently working with the Tanzanians to develop a new compact, built on even more comprehensive sector reforms and intended to establish a more efficient, well-managed power utility that will operate in a competitive market place.

When power is found to be a binding constraint for an MCC partner – which has been the case in Malawi, Tanzania, Ghana, Benin, and Liberia -- MCC works with these governments to identify potential projects to address the nations' inadequate and unreliable power supply. These countries have set ambitious goals and are taking the steps to reform the utility and energy sectors to pave the way for investment and growth. MCC works with host governments, often in coordination with other U.S. Government agencies, most notably through USAID with initiatives such as Power Africa, to help increase technical skills and accelerate energy sector regulatory, market structure and enabling environment reforms that are critical to the expansion and sustainability of the sector and projects.

Although Africa needs approximately $40 billion annually to meet its power needs, only about a third of the investment requirements are currently being met. MCC will help fill a small portion of the investment gap in the sector directly while also helping to leverage significant private sector investments. A reformed and competitive power market, which MCC will also support, should help attract additional private sector investment to fill this gap. In addition to the approximately $1 billion already invested in Malawi, Tanzania and Ghana, MCC plans to invest up to an additional $1 billion in the power sectors of Liberia, Tanzania and Benin

## Current and pending MCC energy investments in Africa

In Ghana, for instance, two main reasons for low levels of private capital in the power sector are the lack of creditworthy off-takers and non-cost-reflective tariffs. To that end, the Public Utilities Regulatory Commission has approved tariffs for the two distribution utilities so that they are moving toward cost-reflectivity. This important step toward cost recovery accompanies a commitment by the government to use an automatic adjustment mechanism to keep the rates reflective of evolving costs. The government has also committed to bring similar order to the pricing and supply of gas – a critical fuel for power generation. In fact, a $16 million component of MCC's compact in Ghana will help the Ghanaians operationalize their "gas-to-power" plan and assist in commercializing the country's gas sector.

As part of the new MCC compact, the Government of Ghana is required to explore and implement private sector participation in the operation of the distribution utility. MCC has also proven the importance of integrating private sector input in program design early on in Ghana's compact development process. In fact, MCC's work scored a significant success when General Electric credited MCC's compact and associated reforms with being a major factor in its plans to build a 1,000 megawatt power park and associated infrastructure in Ghana – a $1.5 billion financial commitment. MCC's Ghana Power Compact has so far been able to catalyze in excess of $4 billion of private sector commitment for the development of the energy sector.

MCC's $350 million compact in Malawi is focused on the turnaround of the power utility and related sector reforms, and strengthening the transmission and distribution infrastructure. The government is taking steps to establish a market-friendly power sector, and the results have been encouraging. A number of key sector reforms have been implemented, the balance sheet of the utility has been cleaned up and the government has agreed to implement a restructuring program to prepare for a competitive power market that includes various options for increasing private sector involvement in the power sector.

As I mentioned, working with other agencies in the Power Africa initiative, MCC will maximize its power sector investments. USAID technical assistance and EXIM and OPIC products can help unlock commercial debt and equity capital, while the use of USTDA studies can reduce the early stage risk for companies.

**The future of energy investments: seeking authority to explore a regional approach**
Moving forward, it has become clear that many of the world's most pressing problems, especially in Africa, are regional, as many private sector participants during the African Leaders' Summit in August 2014 pointed out. I would like to thank members of this committee and subcommittee for their support for efforts to allow MCC to work on a regional basis. In recent years, MCC has identified a number of cases where taking a regional approach would allow us to maximize project benefits and impacts, and the power sector is a good example. Relieving constraints around power often requires a regional approach and the economic impacts of integration in this and other sectors are strong, with the potential to benefit from economies of scale, to support public goods that cross borders, to reduce negative externalities, and to compensate for asymmetries in costs and benefits.

Regionally focused compacts would act as further incentive for countries to facilitate regional and international trade, and would help countries benefit from economies of scale through synergies in sectors such as energy and road infrastructure. We believe a regional approach could be particularly useful in Africa, where markets are fragmented and few countries offer the economies of scale needed for corporate investment

Our ability to fully address regional constraints depends on removing a statutory prohibition on concurrent compacts. Such a change would allow MCC to simultaneously work with multiple countries in a region to identify, negotiate and eventually fund investments that have positive economic effects both for the region and an individual country, while offering the scale that the private sector is seeking. Regionally focused compacts would continue to incentivize improved policy performance, facilitate regional trade and help countries benefit from economies of scale or synergies in sectors such as energy and road infrastructure.

I know that a number of Members of Congress have been supportive of this approach, including Chairman Royce, and Congresswoman Bass has introduced a bill to allow us to achieve this important change.

Finally, I would like to thank you, Chairman Smith, and the other members of the subcommittee for the important support and guidance you have provided for MCC as we have sought to execute on our shared desire to reduce poverty, incentivize reforms and increase private sector-led growth in Africa. As MCC charts a path into our second decade, your support will continue to be crucial to our efforts to fight poverty.

www.ingramcontent.com/pod-product-compliance
Lightning Source LLC
Chambersburg PA
CBHW080315290526
45790CB00005B/2042